EVANGELISM

EVANGELISM

A
CONCISE
HISTORY

LINCOLN CHRISTIAN COLLEGE AND SEMINARY

JOHN MARK TERRY

BROADMAN
& HOLMAN
PUBLISHERS

Nashville, Tennessee

© Copyright • 1994 Broadman & Holman Publishers
All Rights Reserved
4260-44
ISBN: 0-8054-6044-6
Dewy Decimal Classification: 269.2
Subject Headings: EVANGELISTIC WORK
Library of Congress Catalog Number: 93-14446
Printed in the United States of America

Library of Congress-in-Publication Data

Terry, John Mark, 1949-
    Evangelism : a concise history / John Mark Terry.
        p.   cm.
    Includes bibliograpical references.
    ISBN 0-8054-6044-6
    1. Evangelistic work--History.   I. Title
    BV3770.T47   1994   93-14446
    269' .2' 09--dc20   CIP

⇥ CONTENTS ⇤

✣ PREFACE ✣

A chapter in Delos Miles's book, *Introduction to Evangelism*, inspired this book. Reading his chapter on the history of evangelism gave me the idea of writing a longer, fuller treatment of the subject. Many books on the history of missions have been published, but writers have produced surprisingly few books on the history of evangelism.

I wrote this book with students in mind, students in North American colleges and seminaries. Readers looking for an extensive study of this subject should look to sources like Latourette's *History of the Expansion of Christianity*. I tried not to assume too much because students often take a course in evangelism before they take systematic theology and church history. This book is designed as a supplemental text for introductory courses in evangelism or as a text for new courses in the history of evangelism.

I am grateful to several people who helped with the preparation of this book. I am grateful to my professor and mentor, Cal Guy. Vicki Crumpton of Broadman and Holman encouraged me to put together the original proposal. Forrest Jackson, also of Broadman, provided encouragement. I thank my mother for instilling in me a love for history. Finally, I am grateful to my wife, Barbara, and our children, Joanna and Micah, for their patience while I worked on the manuscript.

1

$\approx 1 \approx$

JESUS THE EVANGELIST

The history of evangelism began with the birth of Jesus Christ, the Evangel. Jesus came to earth to be both the Message and the Messenger. The church's later ministry of evangelism drew its inspiration and direction from the evangelism of Jesus. The evangelists of the early church testified to Jesus' life and imitated His methods in their proclamation.

The apostles used the Old Testament Scriptures to demonstrate that Jesus was the fulfillment of prophecies made to the nation of Israel concerning the coming Messiah. They used genealogies to demonstrate that Jesus was a descendant of Abraham and the fulfillment of God's promise to Abraham that "all peoples on earth will be blessed through you" (Gen. 12:3). Jesus' life and work were not historical aberrations but rather a further unfolding of God's plan to redeem the world and restore mankind to fellowship with Himself. In fact, John wrote that Jesus was the "Lamb that was slain from the creation of the world" (Rev. 13:8). Thus the birth of Jesus was part of God's eternal plan of redemption. Truly, the birth of Jesus revealed God's concern for the evangelization of the world and His plan for accomplishing it.

THE PREPARATION FOR THE EVANGEL

Galatians 4:4 says, "But when the time had fully come, God sent his Son." Just as the birth of Christ was not coincidental but

3

part of God's plan, even so the time of Christ's birth was chosen by God. This verse in Galatians does not mean that God sent Jesus when a predetermined date was reached; rather, it means that the circumstances were right for Christ's birth.[1]

God prepared the world to receive Christ when He was born in Bethlehem, about 4 B.C. God sent His Son at a time He had chosen so that His plan of redemption could be fulfilled. Three different nationalities played a part in preparing the world for Jesus' birth. The Greeks prepared the Mediterranean world for Jesus through the spread of their language and culture. When Alexander the Great's army conquered the Middle East in the years 334-323 B.C., Alexander fulfilled not only his dreams of conquest but also his desire to teach the Greek language and culture to the people of that region. Alexander hoped to establish an empire in which the Greek language would bind the diverse peoples together. Death at an early age prevented Alexander from enjoying his success for long, but he did make Greek the common language of the Mediterranean region. The peoples of the region accepted Greek as the language of commerce and education. Anywhere the early evangelists went they were able to preach and witness in Greek. This was a great advantage in their work.

The Greeks also imparted to the Mediterranean world a love for wisdom and learning. The Greek philosophers like Socrates, Plato, and Aristotle exemplified the love of truth and the importance of searching for it. Aristotle had argued for the existence of one God characterized by regularity rather than caprice. Educated people throughout the Roman Empire knew of Aristotle's writings and discussed them. This openness to new ideas was useful to the evangelists of the early church.[2]

The Romans prepared the world for Jesus' birth by establishing peace throughout the Mediterranean region. The Pax Romana (peace of Rome) not only provided an atmosphere of peace and order in which the early church could develop it also made travel much safer for the early missionaries and evangelists. The Romans also unknowingly accelerated the spread of the gospel by building

1. Richard Gist, "The Fullness of Time," *Biblical Illustrator* (Fall 1987), 31.

2. Ibid., 32.

good roads throughout the empire. The Romans built the roads to promote commerce and to speed the deployment of their legions, but these roads also made travel much easier for Paul and the other gospel messengers.

The Jewish people prepared the world for the coming of Christ in several ways. First, when the Jews were scattered throughout the Mediterranean region, they established synagogues in almost every major city. These synagogues became teaching centers that not only were of benefit to the Jews in the community, but also attracted the attention of Gentiles as well. The Book of Acts reveals the presence of Gentile converts to Judaism (prose-lytes) and "God-fearers" (sympathizers) in every synagogue. Second, the Jews prepared the world by spreading the Old Testament throughout the region. When the Old Testament was translated into Greek, the Scriptures became accessible to literate people throughout the area. By disseminating the Old Testament Scriptures and explaining their teachings, the Jews proclaimed their belief in one God (monotheism) and in a coming Savior (the Messiah) who would establish God's kingdom on earth. In this way the Jews established beachheads throughout the Roman Empire that prepared the way for the coming gospel invasion.

The four Gospels provide the information about the way Jesus evangelized people. While one could wish for more information, the Gospels do reveal enough for the reader to understand how Jesus went about this important task.

CHARACTERISTICS OF JESUS' EVANGELISM

PURPOSEFUL

Jesus came with the purpose of winning the world to saving belief in Himself. Jesus stated His purpose again and again. In Luke 19:10 Jesus said, "For the Son of Man came to seek and to save what was lost." In Mark 10:45 Jesus declared, "For even the Son of Man did not come to be served, but to serve, and to give his life as a ransom for many." Though Jesus accomplished this purpose in many different ways, He never lost sight of His singular intent.[3]

---

3. Herschel H. Hobbs, *New Testament Evangelism* (Nashville: Convention Press, 1960), 67.

PERSONAL

Jesus' evangelism was personal in that He dealt with people personally. He did not send a proxy; He came Himself. Jesus' ministry was incarnational. He truly was God in the flesh (John 1:14), and He identified Himself with humanity. Jesus lived as a person. He walked, talked, ate, slept, laughed, and cried with people. He become one with humanity. Jesus could evangelize people because He understood them and spoke their language. Jesus' evangelism was personal also because He dealt with people as individuals. His method was not "one size fits all"; instead, He varied His approach according to the needs of persons and their level of understanding. He began with people where they were and led them to where they needed to be. Jesus' approach with Nicodemus (John 3) was very different from His approach to the woman at the well (John 4). He challenged the rich young ruler (Matt. 19), but He talked gently to the woman taken in adultery (John 8).[4]

POINTED

Jesus called people to salvation, but He also called them to sacrifice and service. Jesus did not hide the cost of discipleship; on the contrary, He offered them a cross to bear and a cup to drink (Mark 8:34-38; 10:38-39). Jesus did not show His followers a broad and easy way; instead, He showed them the narrow way (Matt. 7:13-14). After Jesus fed the five thousand, the people wanted to make Him king (John 6); but when Jesus explained the cost of discipleship, most of those followers left Him. In the parables of the tower builder and the warring king, Jesus explained this fully. Jesus required His disciples to make a well-considered commitment of their lives to Him.[5]

PERENNIAL

Jesus evangelized people in all types of places and at all times of the day. He witnessed to the woman at the well at noon and to

4. Delos Miles, *Master Principles of Evangelism* (Nashville: Broadman Press, 1982), 32.

5. David E. Garland, "Evangelism in the New Testament," *Review and Expositor* (Fall 1980), 462-63.

Nicodemus at night. Jesus met Bartimaeus and Zachaeus beside the road, and He called Peter and John beside the sea. Jesus even witnessed to the thief on the cross. Wherever He went and whenever He could, Jesus presented the gospel.[6]

PERVASIVE

Jesus touched people of every race and social class. Though He came first to tell the good news to the Jews, Jesus demonstrated to His disciples that the gospel was meant for everyone. When Jesus witnessed to the woman at the well and the people of her village, He showed His disciples that the gospel was for Samaritans as well as Jews. When Jesus ministered to the Roman centurion, He ministered to a Gentile. In His last instructions to His disciples, Jesus commanded them to make disciples of "all nations," which could be translated, "all ethnic groups" (Matt. 28:19). In these ways Jesus showed that His salvation was meant for all peoples. Jesus also showed concern for the lowly and outcast. Jesus specifically ministered to women and children (Mark 10:14) and demonstrated His concern for their welfare. Jesus touched a leper and healed him (Mark 1:41). Jesus cast the demons out of the Gadarene demoniac and restored him to wholeness (Luke 8:26-39). Jesus ate and drank with tax collectors like Matthew and Zacchaeus and showed them the way to salvation (Mark 2:14; Luke 19:1-9). Jesus had sympathy and compassion for all types of people. He was open and accepting, seeing people not only for what they were but also for what they could become through God's grace. Through the ministry of Jesus, God's grace pervaded all of society.

PATTERNED

Jesus provided His disciples with a pattern they could follow. Jesus did not just tell the twelve what to do; He modeled evangelism for them. Jesus gave them a living example to follow. He also gave them methods to use that were reproducible. Jesus asked them to do nothing that He had not already demonstrated.

---

6. G. William Schweer, *Personal Evangelism for Today* (Nashville: Broadman Press, 1984), 90.

POWERFUL

His ministry was empowered by the Holy Spirit. Mary conceived Jesus miraculously by the power of the Holy Spirit (Luke 1:35). Jesus began His public ministry after His baptism when the Holy Spirit came upon Him (Matt. 3). On that occasion John the Baptist testified: "I saw the Spirit come down from heaven as a dove and remain on him" (John 1:32). Luke wrote that Jesus was "full of the Holy Spirit" and was "led by the Spirit" (Luke 4:1). After His temptation in the wilderness, Jesus returned to Galilee and ministered in "the power of the Spirit" (Luke 4:14). Jesus cast out demons through the power of the Spirit (Matt. 12:28), and it was through the Holy Spirit that Jesus offered Himself on the cross (Heb. 9:14). Finally, it was the power of the Holy Spirit that raised Jesus from the grave (Rom. 8:11). From beginning to end, Jesus' ministry was permeated and empowered by the Holy Spirit. Jesus depended upon the Spirit's power to make His ministry effective. Even in this He set the example for His disciples.[7]

PRAYERFUL

Jesus maintained His relationship with the Father through prayer. It was Jesus' custom to wake early in the morning in order to pray undisturbed. Jesus prayed at His baptism (Luke 3:21). He prayed before He chose His disciples (Luke 6:12). He prayed before He fed the five thousand (Luke 9:16). He prayed before He raised Lazarus from the tomb (John 11:41-42), and He prayed in the garden before He went to the cross (Luke 22:39-44). Throughout His ministry Jesus relied upon prayer to sustain His power for ministry.

METHODS OF JESUS' EVANGELISM

Jesus used several different methods to communicate the gospel. He was not fixed on one method alone; instead, He varied

---

7. Miles, *Master Principles*, 60. See also Rene Pache's chapter on "The Work of the Holy Spirit in Jesus Christ" in *The Person and Work of the Holy Spirit* (Chicago: Moody Press, 1954).

both His approach and His method according to the circumstances. On many occasions Jesus did *personal* evangelism. In fact, Leighton Ford has identified thirty-five personal interviews recorded in the gospels. In each case Jesus spoke with an individual. Though He often ministered to the masses, Jesus never lost sight of individuals. Jesus found time to talk to Nicodemus, Mary Magdalene, the thief on the cross, and the woman at the well.[8]

JESUS' EVANGELISTIC ACTIONS

In his popular book *How to Give Away Your Faith*, Paul Little pointed out eight significant actions of Jesus in His conversation with the woman at the well (John 4:1-26):

1. *Jesus made contact with the woman.* He initiated the conversation with her. Jesus spoke first.

2. *Jesus established a common ground.* The woman obviously needed water and had come to get some. Jesus, too, needed water, and He asked her to draw some from the well for Him.

3. *Jesus aroused her interest.* When He spoke of "living water" and never thirsting again, Jesus got the woman's attention.

4. *Jesus got the conversation going by asking leading questions and making cryptic statements.*

5. *Jesus did not go too far or too fast with the woman.* He led her along from truth to truth at a pace she could manage.

6. *Jesus did not condemn the woman.* He did not condone her sinful lifestyle, but He did not chastise her for her sin.

7. *Jesus stuck with the main issue.* The woman tried to get Jesus involved in an extended discussion about the proper place to worship, but Jesus refused to pur-

---

8. Leighton Ford, *The Christian Persuader* (New York: Harper & Row, 1966), 67.

sue that topic. He continued to speak to her about eternal life.

8. *Jesus confronted the woman with His claim to be the Messiah, and He challenged her to believe in Him.* Of course, she did, and through her testimony her whole village was saved.[9]

JESUS' EVANGELISTIC LIFESTYLE

Throughout His earthly ministry Jesus demonstrated lifestyle evangelism. Life-style evangelism is evangelism that is done naturally in the daily activities of life. Jesus exemplified this. Jesus spoke to the people He met as He traveled through Palestine. He did not wait to witness until Thursday night visitation. He met blind Bartimaeus on the roadside (Mark 10:46-52) and the Gadarene demoniac on the sea shore. He witnessed to Zaccheus at lunch and to Matthew's friends at supper (Mark 2:15-17). Jesus was opportunistic. He seized every opportunity to share the good news.[10]

JESUS' EVANGELISTIC PREACHING

Preaching was also an important part of Jesus' evangelism. Jesus came preaching like the Old Testament prophets before Him. Indeed, many of the people called him a prophet (Matt. 21:11; Luke 24:19). Jesus was a preacher, not a writer. "Jesus was a voice not a penman, a herald not a scribe, a watchman with his call in the marketplace and the Temple, and not a cry of alarm in the wilderness like John the Baptist."[11] John the Baptist preached to prepare people for the coming of the kingdom of God, but Jesus proclaimed that the kingdom had come. Jesus demonstrated a balanced, threefold ministry of preaching, teaching, and healing (Matt. 4:23). Certainly all three were prominent in His activities,

---

9. Paul Little, *How to Give Away Your Faith*, 2d ed., (Downers Grove, Ill.: InterVarsity Press, 1988), 50-70.

10. Hobbs, *New Testament Evangelism*, 70.

11. Amos Wilder, *The Language of the Gospel* (New York: Harper & Row, 1964), 21.

but Jesus Himself declared that He came primarily to preach. Jesus said, "Let us go somewhere else—to the nearby villages—so I can preach there also. That is why I have come" (Mark 1:38). Although Jesus touched on many different subjects in His preaching, His basic message was simple: "The time has come," He said. "The kingdom of God is near. Repent and believe the good news!" (Mark 1:15). Jesus challenged the people of His day to repent and believe in Him. He not only preached the good news, He was the good news. He presented Himself to the people for acceptance or rejection. [12]

JESUS' EVANGELISTIC TEACHING

Jesus emphasized teaching in His evangelism. For Jesus, "teaching was not merely the recitation of facts. He taught people, not things." [13] His primary concern was to help people understand the nature of God and God's will for their lives. Jesus was a master teacher. He used various methods to help people understand.

Many books have been written on Jesus' way of teaching, but these eight characteristics summarize His approach:

1. *Jesus taught with authority.* The crowds were amazed that Jesus spoke so clearly and without ambivalence (Matt. 7:29).

2. *Jesus taught simply.* He made His teaching simple so that the common people could understand.

3. *Jesus taught by example.* He was a role model. He encouraged His disciples to observe what He did and then imitate it.

4. *Jesus spent time with His disciples.* He gave them time to absorb His teaching and time to observe His way of life and ministry. Jesus demonstrated the principle that evangelism is more often caught than taught.

---

12. Hobbs, *New Testament Evangelism*, 65.
13. Ibid., 66.

5. *Jesus encouraged His disciples to do things for themselves.* After a period of observation Jesus sent them out two-by-two to preach and witness in the villages (Mark 6:7).

6. *Jesus respected the dignity of His disciples.* Jesus was never sarcastic or scornful with His followers.

7. *Jesus showed patience with His disciples.* Even when they were slow to understand or selfish, Jesus corrected them gently.

8. *Jesus used practical illustrations.* Jesus taught in parables. A parable is an extended comparison. Most people comprehend a new thing or idea by comparing it to something familiar. Jesus understood that principle of learning and employed it consistently in His ministry.

Finally, Jesus gave much of His time to *multiplication evangelism.* Jesus spent a lot of time training His twelve disciples to carry on His work. Jesus understood that by multiplying disciples He could grow His church. Robert Coleman in his helpful book, *The Master Plan of Evangelism,* described Jesus' method this way:

> *His concern was not with programs to reach the multitudes, but with men whom the multitudes would follow. . . . Men were to be his method of winning the world to God. The initial objective of Jesus' plan was to enlist men who could bear witness to His life and carry on His work after He returned to the Father.*[14]

JESUS' PRINCIPLES OF TRAINING

Jesus employed several principles as He trained His disciples to carry on His ministry:

---

14. Robert E. Coleman, *The Master Plan of Evangelism* (Old Tappan, N.J.: Fleming H. Revell Co., 1963), 21.

1. *Selection.* Jesus chose men who were seeking for the kingdom of God. He chose men with big hearts who were teachable.

2. *Association.* Jesus spent a lot of time with His disciples. He wanted them to catch His zeal, methods, and spirit.

3. *Consecration.* Jesus expected His disciples to be dedicated and obedient.

4. *Impartation.* Jesus gave Himself away. He gave His time, energy, and knowledge. He sacrificed Himself for His disciples.

5. *Demonstration.* Jesus showed His disciples how to pray, preach, teach, and witness.

6. *Delegation.* Jesus sent them out to evangelize on their own.

7. *Supervision.* Jesus evaluated their ministry and encouraged them. He used review and application to teach new insights.

8. *Reproduction.* Jesus wanted His disciples to reproduce His character and His ministry.[15]

Jesus worked hard at evangelism, but He understood the concept that it is better to train ten men to do the work than it is to do the work of ten men. Jesus knew that His time on earth was limited; therefore, He spent a lot of time equipping His disciples to build His kingdom.

INTERPRETATION AND APPLICATION

Jesus' birth was part of God's plan for world redemption. As such, the birth of Jesus was not coincidental. Instead, Jesus was born at a time when the world was prepared linguistically by the Greeks, politically by the Romans, and religiously by the Jews to

---

15. Ibid., 8.

receive Him. Jesus' evangelism provides a model for modern evangelists to follow.

Jesus was intentional in His evangelism. He came to redeem the lost, and He did not allow Himself to be distracted from that purpose. He accepted all kinds of people and dealt with them as individuals. Jesus challenged the people to count the cost of discipleship. He did not indulge in "easy believism." Most importantly, Jesus demonstrated the necessity of prayer and the power of the Holy Spirit in evangelism.

Jesus used a number of different evangelistic methods. He witnessed to people personally whenever and wherever He could. He preached the good news all over Palestine. He taught the people the way to salvation and challenged them to follow Him. Jesus gave particular attention to training His disciples for their future ministry. Jesus multiplied disciples in order to build the kingdom of God. Jesus began His ministry by calling His disciples to become "fishers of men" (Mark 1:17). He concluded his earthly ministry by commanding His disciples to be witnesses throughout the earth (Acts 1:8).

These two statements by Jesus are like the bookends of His earthly ministry. He came to bring salvation to all peoples, and He commanded His disciples to spread the good news of that salvation. The next chapter describes how the disciples obeyed Jesus' command.

STUDY QUESTIONS

1. How did the Greeks, Romans, and Jews prepare the world for the coming of Christ?

2. What eight words describe Jesus' evangelism?

3. Can you list three examples showing how Jesus ministered to all kinds of people?

4. Why did Jesus use parables so much in His teaching?

5. Why did Jesus spend so much time training His disciples?

6. How should modern evangelism change to conform more closely to Jesus' evangelism?

⊹ 2 ⊹

EVANGELISM IN THE NEW TESTAMENT CHURCH

In His last words to His disciples Jesus commanded them to witness throughout the world. The Book of Acts explains how the church of the New Testament era obeyed that command. Though Luke's account is not exhaustive, it does provide an adequate summary of what the early Christians did. Christians today can study the Acts with profit, discovering principles that should guide evangelism in every age.

THE MESSAGE OF THE NEW TESTAMENT CHURCH

Jesus explained to the apostles what He wanted them to preach before He returned to heaven. "He told them, 'This is what is written: The Christ will suffer and rise from the dead on the third day, and repentance and forgiveness of sins will be preached in his name to all nations, beginning in Jerusalem'" (Luke 24:46-47). This was the basic message proclaimed by the apostles. They preached the death, burial, and resurrection of Jesus and salvation through His name.

One can find examples of the sermons preached in Jerusalem in Acts 2, which records Peter's sermon on the Day of Pentecost, and Acts 7, which contains a sermon by Stephen. In his letter to the Corinthians, Paul explained the essence of his gospel presentation (1 Cor. 15:3-6). Paul built his doctrine on four foundational truths: the deity of Christ, the inerrancy of the Scriptures, the universality of the gospel for both Jews and Gentiles, and the responsibility of the church to spread the gospel. In his preaching Paul emphasized four points: the deity of Christ, Christ's atoning death on the cross, the reality of the resurrection of Christ, and the blessed hope of Jesus' return to earth.[1]

In 1936 C. H. Dodd published a thesis which supported a basic gospel message that was common to all apostolic preaching. Dodd called this basic gospel outline the *kerygma* ("proclamation" in Greek).[2] Dodd believed that the apostolic message included:

A historical account of the death, burial, resurrection, and ascension of Jesus presented as a fulfillment of prophecy; A theological presentation of Jesus as both Lord and Christ (Messiah); A call to repentance and forgiveness of sins.[3]

Scholars in recent years have described Dodd's thesis as an oversimplification. The accepted view today is that the early apostles simply declared the coming of Christ. They adapted their approach according to the nature of their audience. They began where their hearers were intellectually and spiritually and packaged their message in a way that would appeal to the audience. This does not mean they changed the message. It just means that they varied their approach according to the situation. Paul's message to the Greeks assembled on Mars Hill in Athens is a good example of this (Acts 17:22-34). On that occasion Paul preached to philosophers and intellectuals, so he began with a reference to a local religious shrine. However, when Paul addressed the Jewish synagogue in Antioch of Pisidia, he began

1. Roland Q. Leavell, *Evangelism: Christ's Imperative Commission*, rev. ed. (Nashville: Broadman Press, 1979), 59.

2. See C. H. Dodd, *The Apostolic Preaching and Its Development* (London: Hodder and Stoughton, 1936).

3. Robert Mounce, "Gospel," *Baker's Dictionary of Theology* (Grand Rapids: Baker Book House, 1960), 254-57.

with a reference to the Old Testament. Clearly, Paul varied his approach from place to place. In fact, Paul himself testified, "I have become all things to all men so that by all possible means I might save some" (1 Cor. 9:22).[4]

THE STRATEGY OF THE APOSTLES

Acts 1:8 provides a blueprint for the expansion of the early church. In fact, many Bible commentators outline the Book of Acts according to the geographic progression in the verse: Jerusalem, Judea, Samaria, and the ends of the earth. The question, though, is whether this progressive geographic expansion by the church was a conscious strategy on the church's part or simply the leading of the Holy Spirit. Michael Green doubted that the early church had a formal strategy:

> *It would be a gross mistake to suppose that the apostles sat down and worked out a plan of campaign: the spread of Christianity was, as we have seen, largely accomplished by informal missionaries, and must have been to a large extent haphazard and spontaneous.*[5]

More than half of the Book of Acts deals with Paul's missionary efforts. Certainly Paul was the prime human mover in the church's missionary expansion. Therefore, it is important to ask whether Paul had a discernable strategy for evangelizing the Roman Empire. Roland Allen dismissed the idea: "It is quite impossible to maintain that St. Paul deliberately planned his journeys beforehand, selected certain strategic points at which to establish his churches and then actually carried out his designs."[6]

---

4. David E. Garland, "Evangelism in the New Testament," *Review and Expositor* (Fall 1980), 465.

5. Michael Green, *Evangelism in the Early Church* (Grand Rapids: Eerdmans Publishing Co., 1970), 256.

6. Roland Allen, *Missionary Methods: St. Paul's or Ours* (Grand Rapids: Eerdmans Publishing Co., 1962), 10.

Obviously, there is much debate as to whether Paul had a missionary strategy or not. Paul probably did not have an overall, complete plan of action when he began his missionary work. However, if one studies the New Testament carefully, it is possible to discover some basic principles that Paul apparently followed in his efforts to evangelize the Roman Empire. Of course, in all his work Paul was guided by the Holy Spirit.

Herbert Kane has listed nine principles employed by Paul in his work.

1. *Paul maintained close contact with his home church.* The church at Antioch commissioned and sent out Paul and Barnabas on their first missionary journey. After their journey they returned to Antioch to report on their work (Acts 14:26-28).

2. *Paul confined his work primarily to four Roman provinces (Galatia, Asia, Macedonia, and Achaia).* Paul concentrated his efforts in an area small enough for him to provide some supervision and support for the new churches.

3. *Paul concentrated on the large cities.* He established seedbed or mother churches from which the gospel could be spread to the surrounding provinces.

4. *Paul usually began his work in the local synagogue if one existed.* In the synagogues he could share the gospel with Jews, proselytes, and God-fearers who were already looking for the Messiah (Acts 13:14-15).

5. *Paul preferred to preach to responsive peoples.* Paul was determined to be both fruitful and faithful. Therefore, he went where he could achieve good results. He did not waste his time and efforts on unresponsive areas (Acts 18:6).

6. *Paul baptized converts when they made their profession of faith.* It seems that Christian workers in the New Testament era did not require new converts to wait a long time before baptism (Acts 8:12, 36-38; 9:18; 16:33).

7. *Paul remained in one place long enough to establish a church.* He did not sow or plant seed and then leave it unattended.

8. *Paul made good use of his fellow workers by employing a team ministry.* Barnabas, Mark, Silas, Timothy, and Luke accompanied Paul on different missionary journeys. This not only made the work more fruitful, but it enabled Paul to train younger workers.

9. *Paul became all things to all persons.* Paul would not compromise or change his message or doctrine, but he was flexible in other ways. He tried in every way to adapt to the culture in which he was working (1 Cor. 9:19-23).[7]

In summary, then, it is possible to state some general observations about how the early church proceeded with their task of world evangelization. Though these may have not been their predetermined intentions, they were the actions of the church.

1. *The apostles' ministry was inclusive.* The apos- tles evangelized people of all races and nationalities. Though the apostolic church struggled with prejudice, they overcame that and made the church universal (Acts 15; Rom. 1:14; Gal. 3:23).

2. *The apostles emphasized church planting.* They planted churches in key cities in hopes that these churches would spread the gospel into the surrounding area. This strategy succeeded in the case of Thessalonica (1 Thess. 1:8), and it likely did so in other places as well.

3. *The general movement of the church was westward.* Church tradition holds that some of the apostles carried the gospel to the east, and Thomas may have reached India. Still, the primary thrust was to the

---

7. J. Herbert Kane, *Christian Missions in Biblical Perspective* (Grand Rapids: Baker Book House, 1976), 73-85.

west, and Paul dreamed of preaching the gospel as far west as Spain (Rom. 15:24).

4. *The apostolic church confined itself primarily to Greek-speaking areas within the Roman Empire.* There were exceptions to this, of course, but it seems clear that most of the evangelistic work was done where the evangelists could communicate and where they could count on Roman order.

THE HOLY SPIRIT IN THE APOSTLES

The Holy Spirit is so prominent in the Book of Acts that some commentators have suggested calling it the Acts of the Holy Spirit. Jesus knew His disciples could not evangelize the world without the power of the Holy Spirit. That is the reason He told them: "Do not leave Jerusalem, but wait for the gift my Father promised, which you have heard me speak about. For John baptized with water, but in a few days you will be baptized with the Holy Spirit" (Acts 1:4-5). A few moments later Jesus ascended into heaven.

Obedient to their master's command, the disciples returned to Jerusalem and gave themselves to prayer for ten days. On the day of Pentecost they were filled with the Holy Spirit and began to speak in tongues (literally, in dialects). Jerusalem was crowded that day with visitors from all over the Roman Empire. To the amazement of the crowd, the disciples preached in many different languages so that everyone could hear the good news about Jesus in his own language. Peter apparently took the lead in the preaching, and his sermon is recorded in Acts 2. At the conclusion of his message he challenged the people to repent and believe in Christ, and three thousand responded to his invitation. This experience impressed upon the disciples the necessity of the Spirit's power in their evangelistic work.

The Holy Spirit affected the evangelism of the apostolic church in many different ways:

1. *The fullness of the Holy Spirit gave the apostles boldness.* According to Acts 4:31: "After they prayed, the

place where they were meeting was shaken. And they were all filled with the Holy Spirit and spoke the word of God boldly." Some say that the filling of the Spirit causes one to speak in tongues; however, again and again the Book of Acts shows that filling results in bold evangelism.

2. *The Holy Spirit empowered the apostles' preaching (Col. 1:28-29)*. Again and again in the Book of Acts one sees crowds moved by the powerful preaching of the apostles. They were not natural orators; instead, they became supernatural orators when the Spirit empowered them.

3. *The Holy Spirit worked signs and wonders through the early Christians*. These signs and wonders authenticated the message and ministries of the apostles. By means of these miracles the Holy Spirit verified that these men were messengers from God (Acts 4:31; Acts 11:44-47).

4. *The Holy Spirit called out missionaries and evangelists*. Paul explained in Ephesians 4:11 that God called some to serve as apostles, prophets, evangelists, and pastor-teachers. These people were called out and gifted by the Holy Spirit so they could found the church and lead it. Their special responsibility was equipping the church members for ministry. Acts 13:1-3 tells how the Holy Spirit called Paul and Barnabas to serve as missionaries. The Holy Spirit gave the church the leaders it needed in order to carry out its mission.

5. *The Holy Spirit gave spiritual gifts to believers*. Paul explained in 1 Corinthians 12 and 14 how the Holy Spirit gave spiritual gifts to the church members so they could fulfill their role in building up the body of Christ. These gifted believers were a key element in the growth of the early church.

21

6. *The Holy Spirit guided the apostles as they carried out their mission.* In Acts 16:6-10 Luke recounted how Paul wanted to go into the Roman province of Asia and then into Bithynia, but the Holy Spirit prevented him. Finally, Paul went to Troas and sought God's guidance. The Spirit used a dream to reveal to him the open door awaiting him in Macedonia. When Paul and his companions responded to God's leading, they were able to plant churches in Philippi, Thessalonica, and Berea.

In summary, the Holy Spirit was like the propellant that fuels space rockets. With the power of the Holy Spirit the apostles spread the gospel all over the Mediterranean world. The Holy Spirit called them out, inspired their preaching, and guided their travels. As David E. Garland wrote, "They did not preach because they were burdened by the needs of the world or to perpetuate themselves, but because they were spurred by a divine compulsion."[8]

OPPOSITION TO APOSTOLIC EVANGELISM

The early Christians were highly motivated and energized by the Holy Spirit, but they still faced opposition on several fronts. The church's greatest human opposition came from the Jews. Saul and the Sanhedrin led in fierce persecution in Jerusalem that began with the stoning of Stephen (Acts 7:54-8:3). Later, in one of the ironies of church history, Saul (Paul) became the object of Jewish persecution. Paul normally began his ministry in a new city by preaching in the synagogue. Paul knew he would get a hearing there, and the synagogue worshipers accepted the authority of the Scriptures and looked for the coming Messiah. However, as Paul began to make converts the Jews became jealous of his success and began to persecute both Paul and his followers. In many of the cities where Paul evangelized, the Jews incited the people to attack Paul (Acts 13:50; 14:19-20; 17:5-9). This is somewhat ironic in that the Roman authorities

---

8. Garland, "Evangelism in the New Testament," 464.

looked upon Christianity as a sect within the Jewish religion, which had legal recognition. The Jews envied Paul's success because they took great pride in winning converts (proselytes) to Judaism. Then, too, they likely viewed Paul as a turncoat and traitor to their faith.

Idolators also opposed the early evangelists. In some instances idolators viewed Christians as a threat to their religion and to their livelihood. This was the case in Ephesus. A man named Demetrius was one of many silversmiths who made their living making idols of Artemis, the patron goddess of Ephesus. When Paul's evangelistic success began to cut into his sales, Demetrius led a riot against Paul and his companions. Similar situations probably developed in other parts of the Roman Empire as Christianity began to threaten existing religions and those dependent on them.

In the long run the most serious opposition to Christianity came from the Roman authorities. In the beginning Christianity was seen as just another sect of Judaism, and as such Christianity enjoyed legal protection. However, as time passed the Romans came to view Christianity as a separate religion, and thus illegal.

In the early years of the Christian movement Roman persecution was localized. In many cases authorities just reacted to disturbances by punishing those deemed responsible. This was the case at Philippi (Acts 16:22-24), where Paul and Silas were accused of causing a riot. The authorities beat them and imprisoned them until Paul was able to declare his Roman citizenship. In another local persecution, the Romans exiled John to the island of Patmos, and it was there he saw the vision recorded in the Book of Revelation. According to church history, Peter and Paul died when Emperor Nero persecuted the church in Rome itself. Nero blamed the Christians for a terrible fire in Rome and directed a persecution that claimed the lives of many believers. Again, however, this persecution was confined to the city of Rome.

Sometimes the Romans protected the apostles. This was the case in Corinth when Gallio, a Roman magistrate, protected Paul from the Jews (Acts 18). In Jerusalem the Roman soldiers saved Paul's life when he was attacked in the temple (Acts 21:27-35). It seems the Romans were more interested in keeping order in their territories than they were in abstract religious issues.

METHODS OF EVANGELISM

The church of the New Testament era used many different methods to spread the gospel. They were not tied to one particular method; instead, they employed various methods as the situation dictated. Listed below are the methods mentioned in Acts:

1. *Mass evangelism.* The apostles preached the gospel to the masses when they had the opportunity. Peter preached to large crowds in Jerusalem (Acts 2), and Paul preached to a large number at Lystra (Acts 14:8-13).

2. *Public preaching.* Peter and John and the other apostles made it a practice to preach in the temple. Paul preached to Agrippa and other high officials in Caesarea and in Rome itself (Acts 26 and 28).

3. *House-to-house witnessing.* The believers in Jerusalem proclaimed the good news from house to house (Act 5:42). No doubt that is the reason that people were being saved daily (Acts 2:47). The evangelism of family units was an important factor in the growth of Christianity. Normally, when the head of the house accepted Christ, the other members of the household did also. The conversions of Cornelius (Acts 10:23-48) and the Philippian jailor (Acts 16) are good examples of this.[9]

4. *Evangelistic campaigns.* Philip, the preaching deacon, led an evangelistic campaign in Samaria (Acts 8:5). In fact, the results were so good that Peter and John went to Samaria to help with the follow-up (Acts 8:14).

5. *Personal witnessing.* There are many examples of personal witnessing in Acts. Perhaps the best known is

9. Ibid., 469.

Philip's conversation with the Ethiopian eunuch (Acts 8:26-38). Another example is Paul's witness to Sergius Paulus on Cyprus (Acts 13:4-12). C. E. Autrey has suggested that personal witnessing was the normal activity of all Christians in the first century. Acts 11:19 says that some of the believers from Jerusalem who were scattered by the persecution went to Antioch and were "telling" the Jews the good news about the Lord Jesus. The Greek word used here is *lalountes,* which comes from the root word *laleo* (to talk). These witnesses from Jerusalem presented the gospel conversationally to the Jews in Antioch. Their witnessing bore fruit, and a strong church made up of both Jews and Greeks was established in Antioch.[10]

6. *Public debate.* It is hard to know how often this method was used during the New Testament period, but it was used at least once. Acts 17:16-17 tells how Paul discussed the good news with philosophers in Athens.

7. *Lay evangelism.* Much, or perhaps most, of the evangelism was carried on by laymen who witnessed while they went about their daily activities. No doubt they reached many Gentiles who would not have been willing to enter a synagogue. Acts 8:1-4 describes the evangelistic activity of the Christians from Jerusalem who were scattered by persecution. The Jewish hierarchy thought they could destroy the church, but their efforts were as effective as kicking a dandelion. They only succeeded in spreading the gospel throughout the region.[11] The Book of Acts makes it clear that lay evangelism was the rule rather than the exception in the New Testament church. Stephen Neill wrote, "What is clear is that every Christian was a witness. Where there were Christians, there would be a living,

---

10. C. E. Autrey, *Evangelism in the Acts* (Grand Rapids: Zondervan Publishing Co., 1964), 26.16

11. Garland, "Evangelism in the New Testament," 468.

burning faith, and before long an expanding Christian community."[12]

8. *Literary evangelism.* Some of the apostles witnessed with pen and ink. The four Gospels were clearly meant to lead people to faith in Christ. In fact, John stated outright that this was his purpose in writing: "But these are written that you may believe that Jesus is the Christ, the Son of God, and that by believing you may have life in his name" (John 20:31). Luke also shared John's intent (Luke 1:1-4).

9. *Church planting.* The apostles were very church-oriented in their evangelism. They did not just win persons in isolation; rather, they sought to baptize their converts and gather them into congregations for nurture and mutual encouragement. It was Paul's method to establish churches wherever he went, and he stayed long enough to see them established. Later, these churches became mother churches that planted daughter churches.[13]

10. *Home Bible studies.* The early church had no church buildings. They met in homes as well as halls, schools, and the temple. Since they did not rely on formal buildings, the church could multiply as rapidly as Christians made their homes available. Paul used the evangelistic home Bible study effectively in Ephesus to start the church there (Acts 20:20).

INTERPRETATION AND APPLICATION

The message of the early church was simple: Jesus was God's Son who died on the cross to provide salvation to all who believe in Him. After Jesus' ascension the apostles began to tell people about Jesus. The early church did not just *do* mission. As Herbert

---

12. Stephen Neill, *A History of Christian Missions* (Baltimore: Penguin Books, 1964), 24.

13. Garland, "Evangelism in the Early Church," 468.

Kane wrote, "In those early days the church *was* mission. The missionary program of the early church was based on two assumptions: (1) The chief task of the church is world evangelization. (2) The responsibility for carrying out this task rests with the entire Christian community."[14]

The early church probably did not have a formal strategy for evangelizing the world, but their goal was clear. They intended to spread the gospel throughout the Roman Empire. They did this through the power and guidance of the Holy Spirit. They proclaimed the gospel in many different ways, striving to establish new churches. As they worked they faced opposition from Jews, pagans, and the Roman government. Still, by the end of the apostolic era, churches had been established around the Mediterranean rim. This accomplishment is a tribute to the power of the Holy Spirit and the dedication of those early Christians.

The church today could profit from a study of evangelism in the New Testament church. Three things stand out as one examines their work and compares it with modern efforts at evangelism. First, their message was simple. They kept their proclamation so simple that any Christian could share a testimony. Today churches sponsor sixteen-week studies on personal witnessing. These are fine, but witnessing does not have to be that complicated. Second, the early Christians were inspired and guided by the Holy Spirit. The Christians at Jerusalem prayed for ten days and held a one- day crusade. They saw three thousand saved, while many churches today would be delighted with three. Finally, the whole church was active in witnessing. The church today will not grow unless it recovers this emphasis on lay evangelism.

Study Questions

1. What is the gospel? What are the basic truths of the gospel message?

---

14. Kane, *Christian Missions*, 65.

2. What importance did Jesus' words in Acts 1:8 have for the evangelism of the apostles?

3. Why did Paul concentrate his work in cities?

4. What are four characteristics of the early church's evangelism?

5. Why did Jesus caution His disciples to wait for empowering by the Holy Spirit?

6. What methods employed by the early Christians could be used today?

✢ 3 ✢

EVANGELISM IN THE ANCIENT CHURCH

In A.D. 325 Emperor Constantine welcomed 318 bishops to the Council of Nicea. These bishops represented churches from Spain in the West to Persia in the East. How did the church grow from the small group that met in the upper room in Jerusalem to the impressive institution reflected at Nicea?

CHURCH GROWTH TO A.D. 100

Church historians normally date the end of the Apostolic Age at A.D. 95-100. This corresponds to the date of the death of the apostle John. When John died, the age of the apostles ended. What was the state of the church at that time? A careful reading of Acts and the Epistles reveals that there were already clusters of churches in Palestine and Asia Minor, especially in western Asia Minor. Paul planted many of those churches on his first and second missionary journeys, as well as other churches in Macedonia, Achaia, and Cyprus. Titus evangelized the island of Crete, and unknown Christians founded the church at Rome. It seems there was a church at Puteoli near Naples because Paul stayed with Christians there while on his way to Rome (Acts 28:13-14).

According to the ancient traditions of the church, Thaddaeus preached in Edessa; Mark founded the church at Alexandria; Peter preached in Bithynia; Thomas witnessed in India; and Paul carried the gospel as far as Spain. All of these traditions are not verifiable;

29

but even if one accepts them, it is clear that the number of churches in A.D. 100 was still quite small—perhaps no more than one hundred congregations. Also, the existing churches were limited in size. The churches at Jerusalem, Antioch, Ephesus, and Rome seem to have had large memberships, but the other churches were rather small.

Most of the churches were located in urban areas. This was because Paul and his associates primarily worked in the cities of the Roman Empire. In fact, the English word, "pagan," comes from the Latin *pagani,* which means "those who live in the country-side." The rural people were the last to hear and accept the gospel.

The urban churches worshiped in Greek for the most part. Of course, in the early years the church reflected a strong Jewish influence; however, with the success of Paul's missionary work among the Gentiles and the destruction of the Jerusalem Temple in A.D. 70, the churches became more and more Hellenistic. Thus, the New Testament was written in Greek, as were most Christian documents of the second century. At the end of the Apostolic Age one could say that the church was limited in size, mainly urban, and spoke primarily Greek.[1]

The history of the early church is usually divided into two periods, Ante-Nicene and Post-Nicene. These terms refer to an important church council which met at Nicea in A.D. 325. Ante-Nicene refers to things before 325, and Post-Nicene to things that happened after 325.

During the second century of Christianity the church spread naturally along the main roads and rivers of the Empire. As missionaries and evangelists followed these natural travel routes, they carried the gospel eastward into Arabia and Persia; westward through Alexandria into North Africa; and northward into Armenia, Pontus, and eventually to Gaul (France) and Britain.[2]

---

1. Timothy George, "The Challenge of Evangelism in the History of the Church," in *Evangelism in the Twenty-First Century,* ed. Thom Rainer (Wheaton, Ill.: Harold Shaw, 1989), 10.

2. Herbert Kane, *A Global View of Missions* (Grand Rapids: Baker Book House, 1975,) 10.

Egypt and North Africa became strongholds of Christianity during the second century. The churches in North Africa were the first Latin-speaking churches. They appealed primarily to the upper classes in cities and towns. During this period the villages were still untouched.[3]

The church in Asia Minor grew rapidly during the second century. In fact, Pliny, a Roman official, wrote to Emperor Trajan in A.D. 112 about the Christians in Bithynia. He complained that "there are so many people involved in the danger. . . . For the contagion of this superstition has spread not only through the free cities, but into the villages and rural districts . . ." Pliny went on to report that "many persons of all ages and both sexes" were involved. Obviously, the Christians in Bithynia were multiplying, and this seems to have been true in and around Ephesus as well.[4] The church at Rome also grew during this period, in both size and prestige, until by A.D. 251 the church included 46 presbyters (pastors), 7 deacons, 7 sub-deacons, 42 clerks, and 52 exorcists, readers, and janitors.[5]

Kenneth Scott Latourette estimated that by the end of the second century Christians could be found in all the provinces of the Roman Empire as well as in Mesopotamia. This seems to be an accurate assessment in light of this statement by Tertullian to the pagans: "We have filled every place belonging to you, cities, islands, castles, towns, assemblies, your very camp, your tribes, companies, palace, senate, forum! We leave you your temples only!" Tertullian may have exaggerated somewhat, but it does seem clear that the church penetrated every part of Roman society by A.D. 200[6]

---

3. Stephen Neill, *A History of Missions* (Baltimore: Penguin Books, 1964), 36.

4. "Pliny to Trajan," in *Documents Illustrative of the History of the History of the Church*, 3 vols., ed. B. J. Kidd (London: Society for Promoting Christian Knowledge, 1920), 1:39.

5. Eusebius Pamphilus, *Ecclesiastical History* 4:43, trans. C. F. Cruse (Grand Rapids: Baker Book House, 1984), 265.

6. Kenneth Scott Latourette, *A History of the Expansion of Christianity*, 7 vols. (New York: Harper & Brothers, 1937), 1:85.

What kind of people became Christians in the second century? There is very little information about this. Some were wealthy, and some were poor. Some like Tertullian were well educated, while many were uneducated. The difficulty lies in determining the ratios. There is one clue in an accusation made by an anti-Christian writer named Celsus:

> *Their aim is to convince only worthless and contemptible people, idiots, slaves, poor women, and children. They behave like mountebanks and beggars; they would not dare to address an audience of intelligent men. . . . but if they see a group of young people or slaves or rough folk, there they push themselves in and seek to win the admiration of the crowd. It is the same in private houses. We see wool-carders, cobblers, washermen, people of the utmost ignorance and lack of education. . . . if they manage to get children alone, or women as senseless as themselves, then they set to work to put forth their wondrous tales. These are the only ones whom they manage to turn into believers.*[7]

Celsus was hardly an unbiased witness, but one can infer from his statement that most of the Christians came from the lower or working classes. This is a normal thing sociologically. Most new religious movements have found their first converts among the disadvantaged folk in society. Also, the fact that Christianity was viewed as an illegal religion by the Roman government discouraged more prominent citizens from becoming involved.

Christianity grew steadily but not dramatically from 200 until A.D. 260. Then the church grew very rapidly until Emperor Diocletian's edict of persecution in A.D. 303. Up until A.D. 260 the church had been a mainly urban institution, but in the last

---

7. Origen, *Against Celsus* 3:49-55 in *The Ante-Nicene Fathers*, eds. Alexander Roberts and James Donaldson (Grand Rapids: Eerdmans Publishing Co., 1951), 4:484-86.

forty years of the third century many rural people became Christians. This movement of the rural masses was prompted by civil strife in the Roman Empire and accompanying economic depression. This was the period of the "barracks emperors," and the civil government was in chaos much of the time. The resulting economic problems made life very difficult for the rural folk. As a result, many farm families began to question their traditional religion as the hard times continued.

The Christians preached a simple gospel that offered both social justice and assurance of power over demonic forces. Thousands, perhaps millions, gave up their old gods and accepted Christ. This was the greatest time of growth in the ante-Nicene period. It was made possible in part because the church was free from persecution for those forty years. The civil government was occupied with other matters during that time.[8]

This great period of peace and progress ended when Emperor Diocletian issued his edict of persecution in A.D. 303. This terrible persecution lasted until Constantine gained the throne in A.D. 311. During this period many Christians died as martyrs and others were tortured. Lasting peace came when Constantine issued his edict of toleration in 311 and his famous Edict of Milan in A.D. 313.

By A.D. 300 evangelists had preached the gospel in every city and province of the Empire. However, the distribution of churches was very uneven. The church had grown more rapidly in Syria, Asia Minor, Egypt, and North Africa. Growth in other areas—Gaul, for example—had been slow. Harnack believed that in one or two provinces in Asia Minor at least half the people were Christians. He estimated the number of Christians in the Empire at three or four million at the beginning of Constantine's reign.[9]

Under Constantine's rule the number of Christians increased rapidly. When he made Christianity the favored religion, church

---

8. W. H. C. Frend, *The Early Church* (Philadelphia: Fortress Press, 1982), 110-11.

9. Adolf Harnack, *The Mission and Expansion of Christianity in the First Three Centuries*, 2 vols., trans. James Moffatt (New York: G. P. Putnam's Sons, 1908), 2:325.

memberships swelled, although the quality may have declined in proportion. Still, the church made remarkable progress between A.D. 100 and 325. The question remains—how did the church grow?

THE METHODS OF THE ANTE-NICENE CHURCH

ITINERANT EVANGELISTS

From its beginning Christianity has been a missionary religion. The evangelists of the second and third centuries followed the example set by the apostles in the first century. Eusebius wrote the history of the early church, and he reported that there were itinerant missionaries in the second century who evangelized in much the same way as Paul.

> *For most of the disciples at that time, animated with a more ardent love of the divine word, had first fulfilled the Saviour's precept by distributing their substance to the needy. Afterwards leaving their country, they performed the office of evangelists . . . [and] also delivered to them the books of the holy gospels. After laying the foundation of the faith in foreign parts . . . [t]hey went again to other regions and nations, with the grace and cooperation of God. The Holy Spirit also wrought many wonders as yet through them, so that as soon as the gospel was heard, men voluntarily in crowds, and eagerly, embraced the true faith with their whole minds . . .[10]*

The *Didache*, a Christian document of the second century, also mentions itinerant "apostles and prophets" in need of hospitality. Origen, a third-century writer, wrote of evangelists of his time: "Some of them have made it their business to itinerate, not

---

10. Eusebius, (3:37), 123.

only through cities, but even villages and country houses, that they might make converts to God." So it seems clear that itinerant evangelists remained active in the second and third centuries.[11]

Evangelistic Bishops

The bishops of the early church considered it their responsibility to administrate the church and continue the apostles' evangelistic mission. The bishops of large city churches led in the evangelization of the surrounding countryside. Some churches ordained bishops and sent them into unevangelized areas to win people to Christ and organize churches.

Irenaeus and Gregory Thaumaturgos are good examples of missionary bishops. Irenaeus (ca. A.D. 130-200) served as bishop of Lyons in what is now France. He actively evangelized the pagan tribes that lived near Lyons. Gregory became bishop of a town in Pontus about A.D. 240. When he became bishop there were only seventeen members of his church, but when he died there were only seventeen pagans left in the city. The numbers may be exaggerated, but clearly Gregory was quite successful in his evangelistic efforts. He exposed pagan miracles as frauds and performed so many wonders himself that he became known as Gregory Thaumaturgos (worker of wonders).[12]

Lay Evangelists

Though missionaries and bishops set good examples in evangelism, laymen did most of the evangelism in the early church. They shared the gospel while they went about their daily activities. It is easy to imagine laymen conversing with their friends in their homes, at the market, and on street corners. In fact, Celsus complained about this very practice in the quotation cited above.[13]

---

11. *The Didache* in *The Early Christian Fathers*, ed. Henry Bettenson (New York: Oxford University Press, 1956), 71.

12. Neill, *History of Missions*, 34, and Latourette, *History of Expansion*, 1:89-90.

13. Michael Green, *Evangelism in the Early Church* (Grand Rapids: Eerdmans Publishing Co., 1970), 173.

Christians also shared the gospel as they traveled throughout the Empire. Christian merchants evangelized as they traveled, much as did the Christians scattered from Jerusalem (Acts 8:4). Believers who served in the Roman army witnessed wherever they were stationed. Some scholars believe Roman soldiers first brought the gospel to Britain. The Roman government pensioned retiring soldiers with a plot of land in a new territory. These retired soldiers sometimes established churches in remote places. This was definitely the case in southeastern Europe.[14]

Women played a major role in the growth of the early church. Harnack wrote, "The equalizing of man and woman before God (Gal. 3:28) produced a religious independence among women, which aided the Christian mission." Since the early churches normally met in homes, many women were able to make their homes house-churches. Also, many women died bravely as martyrs and thus gave a testimony for Christ.[15]

PUBLIC PREACHING

Peter and Paul often preached in public, and this practice continued in the second and third centuries as conditions permitted. Eusebius records that Thaddaeus preached in Edessa saying, "Since I was sent to preach the word, summon for me tomorrow an assembly of all your citizens, and I will preach before them and sow in them the word of life." These early preachers proclaimed the gospel so as to bring their listeners to repentance and belief in Christ. They confronted them with the crisis of decision.[16]

TEACHING

Teaching was another method of evangelism employed by the early church. The early catechetical schools (schools for church teachers) developed into training schools for pastors in Antioch, Alexandria, and other places. All of these schools sent

---

14. W. O. Carver, *The Course of Christian Missions* (New York: Fleming H. Revell Co., 1932), 51.

15. Harnack, *The Mission and Expansion*, 2:64-65.

16. Eusebius, 1:13, 47.

out evangelists and missionaries. The teachers at the schools evangelized both their students and the surrounding communities. Pagans as well as student-pastors attended these schools. Origen, a teacher at Alexandria, won Gregory Thaumaturgos to Christ while Gregory was a student.[17]

HOUSEHOLD EVANGELISM

The early Christians used their homes to spread the gospel. Because there were no church buildings for almost two hundred years, the congregations met in one or several homes. The home setting provided a relaxed, unthreatening atmosphere. The warm hospitality offered by Christian homes no doubt influenced many. Then, too, whole households were sometimes converted, as was true of the Philippian jailor's family (Acts 16). The New Testament contains many references to house or home churches, and this practice was continued by the early church.[18]

LITERARY EVANGELISM

Most early Christians witnessed by means of preaching and personal testimony; however, the documents of the early church reveal that Christians also shared their faith through literature. Literary evangelism included apologies (defenses of the faith), letters, polemics (attacks on heresy), and the distribution of the Scriptures themselves. W. O. Carver believed that all of the ante-Nicene Fathers "were in varying degrees missionaries of the pen." Justin Martyr wrote his *Second Apology* with the stated intention that his readers would be converted. No doubt other writers shared this purpose, whether it was stated or not.[19]

PERSONAL EXAMPLE

The early Christians often spread the gospel through the testimony of their daily lives. Their personal conduct and example influenced many to come to Christ. Justin Martyr wrote of this:

---

17. Carver, *Christian Missions*, 50-51.
18. Green, *Early Church*, 207.
19. Carver, *Christian Missions*, 47-50.

He has urged us . . . to convert all . . . and this I can show to have taken place with many that have come in contact with us, who were overcome, and changed from violent and tyrannical characters, either from having watched the constancy of their neighbor's lives or from having observed the wonderful patience of fellow travelers under unjust exactions, or from the trial they made of those with whom they were concerned in business.[20]

The conduct of Christians during times of persecution also influenced many pagans. Although some did deny Christ under torture, many gave wonderful testimonies. When threatened with death by burning at the stake, Polycarp of Smyrna declared: "Eighty and six years have I served him, and he never did me wrong; and how can I now blaspheme my King that has saved me?" Roman persecution did not destroy Christianity; rather, it strengthened it. The blood of the martyrs really did prove to be the seed of the church.[21]

SOCIAL SERVICE

The early Christians won others to Christ through social service. Adolf Harnack listed ten different ministries performed by the Christians: alms in general, support of teachers and officials, support of widows and orphans, support of the sick and infirm, the care of prisoners and convicts in the mines, the burial of paupers, the care of slaves, providing disaster relief, furnishing employment, and extending hospitality. It seems clear that these benevolent activities affected evangelism positively because the pagan emperor, Julian the Apostate (A.D. 332-363), complained about it:

[Christianity] has been especially advanced through the loving service rendered to strangers,

---

20. Justin, *Apology*, 1:16, in Kidd, *Documents*, 1:74.
21. Eusebius, 4:15, 147.

and through their care for the burial of the dead. . .. The godless Galileans care not only for their own poor but for ours as well.[22]

CHURCH GROWTH, A.D. 325-500

The post-Nicene church grew in an environment very different than it knew before. Until the Edict of Milan in A.D. 313 the church developed amidst persecution and opposition. However, with the toleration and favor granted by Emperor Constantine, new members flooded the churches. The clear insincerity of many new church members caused the development of the monastic movement. Monastic communities played a major role in the church's expansion in this period.

The church also had to adjust to the decay of the Roman Empire. As the Empire's power declined, pagan tribes began to move into territories previously controlled by the Romans. The church faced the daunting challenge of evangelizing these tribes and incorporating them into churches. When the tribes captured Rome itself, the church had to deal with them at close quarters.

By the time of the Council of Nicea in A.D. 325, Christians were still a minority group in the Empire. Stephen Neill has estimated that they comprised no more than ten percent of the population. The church was strong in Asia Minor, Palestine, and North Africa. However, the church was still weak in southern Italy, Sicily, Greece, and in many rural areas.

It is easier to characterize Christianity at A.D. 325 than it is to estimate the number of believers. Generally speaking, Christianity was stronger in Greek-speaking areas than in the provinces where Latin was the primary language. This was a natural result because most of the missionaries and evangelists were Greek-speaking and the Scriptures were in Greek. The churches were also predominantly urban. This was the result of the missionary methods employed by the church, which had concentrated its evangelistic efforts in the cities and the natural conservatism of the peasants. Finally, most Christians were from

---

22. Neill, *History of Missions*, 42.

the lower and middle classes. The wealthy were slow to respond, especially while Christianity was still an illegal religion and was viewed as a threat to the status quo.[23]

EVANGELISTIC METHODS

As one would expect, the post-Nicene church employed most of the same methods that proved so effective earlier. However, the changing circumstances in the Empire and the church required some changes in the church's methodology.

EVANGELISTIC BISHOPS

Probably many bishops enjoyed evangelistic success during this period, but four names stand out: Ulfilas, Martin of Tours, Ambrose of Milan, and John Chrysostom.

Ulfilas as the great missionary to the Goths. Although the Goths had heard the gospel from Christian traders and captives, Ulfilas was the one who evangelized this large tribe. He preached to the Goths for thirty-seven years and translated much of the Bible into the Gothic language.

Martin of Tours (316-397) was a saintly and evangelistic bishop who influenced many for Christ. He had lived as a monk and loved life in the monastery so much that he continued to live in a monastery even after he became a bishop. As bishop, Martin traveled widely throughout Gaul and won thousands of converts by his preaching and miracles. He had particular success in the rural areas.

Ambrose of Milan is remembered for his outstanding preaching and influence on Augustine of Hippo. Ambrose served for many years as bishop of Milan, and he won many pagans there through his powerful preaching. He also encouraged the evangelization of the people living in the Alps.

John Chrysostom (347-407) was bishop of Constantinople and one of the great preachers of all time. In fact, his name

---

23. A. H. M. Jones, "The Social Background of the Struggle Between Paganism and Christianity," in *Paganism and Christianity in the Fourth Century*, ed. A. Momigliano (London: Oxford University Press, 1963), 17.

means "golden-mouthed." John wrote an apologetic with the aim of winning pagans and Jews. He also sent missionaries into several pagan areas.

MONASTICISM AND EVANGELISM

Monasticism developed as a reaction to the decline of morals and dedication in the churches. This was brought on in part by the favor of the emperors toward Christianity after the time of Constantine. When it became politically expedient to be a Christian, many joined the church. Unfortunately, many of these new members had not been born again. They maintained their pagan attitudes and much of their pagan life-style. In reaction, many dedicated Christians sought to find pure Christianity in isolated places such as deserts and the mountains. As the number of these hermits increased, they formed communities which became known as monasteries.

The monks that joined the monasteries lived in a tension between their desire to live away from the world and Christ's command to evangelize the world. Many monks tried to resolve this tension by spending time in the monastery and then going out on preaching missions for a time. When monks were ordained as priests, it was usually for the purpose of doing missionary work. Some of the most effective evangelists of the post-Nicene period were missionary monks. Then, too, many monasteries were established with the idea that they would win the people of the surrounding area to Christ. Though the great days of monastic evangelism lay in the future, it is important to acknowledge the work of the monks in this age as well.

INDIVIDUAL EVANGELISTS

As in the period before A.D. 325, individual missionaries continued to itinerate after Nicea. Philaster, who was called a "second Paul," traveled throughout the Empire preaching to pagans and Jews. He carried on a notable evangelistic work in Rome itself and eventually became the bishop of Brixia.[24]

---

24. Latourette, *History of Expansion*, 1:186.

The most famous of the missionaries of this era is Patrick of Ireland. Patrick (389-461) was born in Britain and raised in a Christian home. When he was sixteen, he was captured by a band of marauders and taken to Ireland. He lived as a slave for six years. Eventually he returned to Britain, but he had a vision which he interpreted as a divine call to preach in Ireland.

Patrick preached in Ireland for more than thirty years. In his *Confession* he told of baptizing thousands. He tried to win the local rulers and through them reach the masses, but this was not always successful. Though he was not the first to preach in Ireland, he converted many districts to Christ and brought Ireland into relationship with the Roman Church.[25]

LAY EVANGELISM

Lay evangelists played an essential part in the expansion of Christianity after Nicea just as they did before. Captives, soldiers, and merchants all witnessed for Christ as they had opportunity. Frend said, "The Christian merchant of this period was the propagator of his faith as the Moslem merchant has been in more recent centuries."[26]

The kingdom of Axum (Abyssinia) was won to Christ through the witness of two young travelers, Aedessius and Frumentius. Captured by the Abyssinians, they impressed the king and became the stewards of his household. The two young Christians held regular worship services and invited both visiting traders and local folk to attend. After some years they obtained permission to return to their home country.

Aedessius returned to Tyre, their hometown, but Frumentius went to Alexandria to report their activities to Bishop Athanasius. When Athanasius heard this remarkable story, he said, "Who better than yourself can scatter the mists of ignorance and introduce among this people the light of divine preaching?" Athanasius

---

25. J. B. Bury, *The Life of St. Patrick and His Place in History* (London: Macmillan Co., 1905) 212.

26. Frend, *Early Church*, 240.

immediately consecrated Frumentius as a bishop and sent him back to Abysinnia, where he worked diligently.[27]

INTERPRETATION AND APPLICATION

It is important to ask the question—Why did the church grow? What made their evangelism so successful?

1. *The church grew because of divine blessing.* God blessed the efforts of the early Christians. The early church was the instrument of the Holy Spirit in fulfilling the redemptive purpose of God.

2. *The church grew because Christians were zealous.* They sacrificed themselves for the faith. The early Christians possessed a burning conviction that expressed itself in evangelistic activity.

3. *The church grew because the gospel was appealing.* Latourette believed the uniqueness of Christianity was the key. The simple monotheism of Christianity combined with its high ethical standards was attractive indeed.[28]

4. *The church grew because of its organization and discipline.* The bishops took the lead in evangelism and missions, and they held the church together during times of persecution. Also, the strict discipline of the church presented a marked contrast to the pagan cults.

5. *The church grew because of its inclusiveness.* It attracted people of all classes and races. It became a universal religion. It burst the restrictive bonds of Judaism to become a true world religion.

27. Theodoret, *Ecclesiastical History*, trans. E. Walford (London: H. G. Bond, 1854), 1:22.
28. Latourette, *History of Expansion*, 1:168.

6. *The church grew because of its members' life-style.* The early believers were not perfect, but their lives were much different from their pagan neighbors. Their faithfulness in the face of persecution and their many acts of charity attracted many to Christ.

7. *The church grew because it worked at growing.* The early believers were not content with the status quo. They wanted the church to grow and expand into new areas. Bishops, clergy, and laity alike shared the gospel wherever they went.

STUDY QUESTIONS

1. What role did laymen play in the growth of the ancient church?

2. What characteristics of Christianity appealed to the people of the Roman Empire?

3. What role did women play in the growth of the ancient church?

4. What evangelistic methods did the ancient church employ?

5. How did social ministry affect the evangelistic work of the ancient churches?

6. How is the environment of America in the twentieth century like and unlike the environment of Christianity in the Roman Empire?

─4─

EVANGELISM IN THE MIDDLE AGES

The Middle Ages lasted from A.D. 500 until about A.D. 1500 Historians once called this era the "Dark Ages" because they considered the period a cultural desert. Historians now recognize the Middle Ages as a time of slow but constant change. During this period the Roman Catholic Church took shape and became the dominant social and political institution in Europe. In fact, the Roman Church so dominated the lives of people in western Europe that many historians call this period the "Age of Faith." It was not a dark age for evangelism.

In 500 A.D. Christianity was the major religion of the Roman Empire, but many areas and tribes within the former boundaries of the Empire remained unevangelized. Many of these were Germanic peoples who migrated into areas formerly controlled by the Romans. They established their own kingdoms and took by force whatever land and property they wanted. This influx hastened the collapse of the Roman Empire, but it did not cause the collapse of the Roman Church; instead, the church filled the vacuum left by the collapse of the Roman government. The popes in Rome and other church leaders acted as quickly as possible to bring these tribes into the church. In addition, the church sought the conversion of northern Europe and Scandinavia, areas still largely untouched by the gospel. By A.D. 1500 , however, Europe was thoroughly Christianized. How did the church spread the gospel during this period? How did the church achieve this remarkable progress?[1]

EVANGELISM THROUGH MONASTICISM

The major force in evangelism in the Middle Ages was monasticism. The monasteries played a great part in the Christianization of Europe. Monasticism developed as a reaction to the decline of morality in the church. Individual Christians went to isolated areas to separate themselves from the world and seek God. As time passed, hermits joined together to form communities which devoted themselves to prayer and meditation. These communities grew to the point where more organization was necessary. These standardized communities came to be called monasteries. In the latter Middle Ages several orders of traveling monks were established, most notably the Franciscans and Dominicans. These monks spent much of their time traveling and preaching. In the beginning they lived only on the food the local people gave them.

The great organizer of monasticism was Benedict of Nursia, considered the patriarch of Western monasticism. In 529 Benedict founded a monastery at Monte Cassino near Rome. Benedict developed a set of rules to order the lives of his fellow monks. His rules followed four emphases:

1.   *Organization.* Each monastery was governed by an abbot.

2.   *Vows.* Each monk took vows of poverty, chastity, and obedience.

3.   *Exercise.* Each monk was expected to worship, work, and study according to a strict schedule.

4.   *Simplicity.* The monks were expected to strive for simplicity in every area of life.[2]

---

1. Milton L. Rudnick, *Speaking the Gospel Through the Ages* (St. Louis: Concordia Publishing House, 1984), 43.
2. "Benedict of Nursia," *The Wycliffe Biographical Dictionary of the Church* (Chicago: Moody Press, 1982), 38.

During the ten centuries of the Middle Ages the monastic movement went through periods of decline and renewal. Rudnick pointed out that monasticism was a good reflection of the church's health. When monasticism prospered, so did the Roman Catholic Church; when it declined, the church suffered.[3]

Monasticism developed through four stages of religious life:

1. *Eremitic monasticism* (hermits).

2. *Cenobitic monasticism* (communities).

3. *Monastic orders* (practical, organized, related to other monasteries).

4. *Mendicant orders* (friars who traveled and preached).

Monasticism was important for several reasons. First, the monasteries served as repositories for western culture. Each monastery had a library, and these libraries protected and preserved important ancient documents and artifacts. Second, the monasteries were centers of education. All new monks learned to read and write, and in some places during the early Middle Ages the monks were the only people who could read. Third, the monks provided the church with a highly disciplined force of trained preachers and evangelists. Again and again, the popes and bishops called on the monks to spearhead the church's advance into new areas.

Usually, the monks penetrated a new area by asking permission from a local ruler to establish a monastery. After gaining this permission, the monks would build temporary shelters and begin their normal routine of worship, prayer, study, and work. Their piety and good character usually attracted the curiosity of the local residents. The monks soon converted some of the interested onlookers. After establishing a good reputation in the area, the monks began to visit the local villages to preach and teach. Soon new churches ringed the monastery, and the monks pastored the churches until a bishop could organize the churches in the area.[4]

---

3. Rudnick, *Speaking the Gospel*, 49.
4. Ibid., 68.

One outstanding example of monastic evangelism was the work of Columba (521-597). In his early years Columba lived as a monk in Ireland. He founded several monasteries, just as Patrick had done. In 563 Columba took twelve fellow monks and founded a new monastery on the island of Iona near the coast of Scotland. The monastery at Iona was a base from which to evangelize the Picts, a tribe in northern Scotland. Even after Columba's death, the monastery at Iona continued to send out evangelists. One monk won a prince named Oswald to faith in Christ. When Oswald returned home to Northumbria, he asked the monastery to send a missionary to evangelize his people. The abbot sent Aidan, who not only evangelized the people of Northumbria but also founded a new monastery modeled after the one at Iona.[5]

The church also used monasteries to win the people of what is now Holland and Belgium. Willibrord (658-739) was a monk who was supported by Pepin II, king of the Franks. At Pepin's request Willibrord took twelve monks and founded a monastery at Utrecht. This Benedictine monastery became the mother of monasteries at Antwerp, Echternach, and Susteren. Monks from these four monasteries evangelized the people of the region and made the monasteries the church's beachhead.[6]

EVANGELIZATION BY MISSIONARIES

In the Middle Ages, as in every era, individual evangelists made a great difference in the church's expansion.

AUGUSTINE OF CANTERBURY

One such evangelist was Augustine. Augustine (not the famous African bishop) was sent by Pope Gregory the Great to evangelize Britain in 596. At that time some Christian churches already existed in Britain, but they were not under the supervision of Rome. Pope Gregory ordered Augustine to gather a group

---

5. M. Thomas Starkes, *God's Commissioned People* (Nashville: Broadman Press, 1984), 65-66.
6. Ibid., 69.

of monks and bring the Anglo-Saxons of southeastern England into the Roman fold. Like Jonah of Old Testament times, Augustine accepted the assignment with great reluctance; when his band of missionaries encountered difficulties along the way, he asked to be relieved of his assignment. Pope Gregory insisted that Augustine and his companions continue, and they finally arrived in England. Although the king was afraid of the monks at first, fearing they would cast a spell upon him, he allowed the band to settle in Canterbury. From this base Augustine converted not only the king but ten thousand of his subjects as well. Eventually, the pope appointed Augustine as the first archbishop of Canterbury. Through Augustine's influence, English Christians became part of the Roman Catholic Church.[7]

Augustine and his companions won the loyalty of the king and his people for several reasons. They preached fervently with great conviction. Queen Bertha was a Christian and supported their mission. They followed the instructions of Pope Gregory and accommodated Catholicism to the old religion of the people. Pope Gregory wrote them:

> *The heathen temples of these people need not be destroyed, only the idols which are to be found in them. . . . If the temples are well built, it is a good idea to detach them for the worship of the true God . . . . And since the people are accustomed, when they assemble for sacrifice, to kill many oxen in sacrifice to the devils, it seems reasonable to appoint a festival for the people by way of exchange.*[8]

Augustine cast the idols out of the pagan shrines, purified the buildings with holy water, and changed them into churches. He also changed the ancient festivals into feasts that honored Christian saints. Because of this, some assert that Augustine's

---

7. Ibid., 67.

8. Stephen Neill, *A History of Missions* (Baltimore: Penguin Books, 1964), 68.

brand of Christianity was only a veneer over the traditional religion of the people.[9]

BONIFACE

One of the most famous medieval evangelists was Boniface (680-754). A disciple of Willibrord, he lived in the monastery until he was forty years old. He began his evangelistic ministry among the people of Frisia, but in 722 Pope Gregory II called him to Rome and appointed him bishop of the German peoples.[10]

When Boniface returned from Rome, he worked first among the people of Hesse, in what is now Germany. At first he won few converts, but Boniface achieved a great breakthrough by means of a power encounter. Boniface learned that most of the people of the area worshiped at the sacred oak of Thor at Geismar. The people believed their god Thor would destroy anyone who desecrated the oak. Like Elijah on Mount Carmel, Boniface chopped down the oak. The people waited for Thor to strike down Boniface. When nothing happened to him, the people shouted, "The Lord, he is God." Boniface took the wood from the tree and built a chapel. By means of this power encounter Boniface demonstrated God's power to the superstitious Hessians. Thereafter, Boniface, through his preaching and confrontations, established Christianity as the dominant religion in the area.[11]

After his signal success at Geismar, Boniface went on to evangelize the people of Bavaria and Thuringia as well. Courageously he preached, destroyed pagan shrines, and founded churches and monasteries. Eventually, he was named archbishop of Mainz, and he used his new position to work for reforms in the church. At age seventy-eight he resigned his bishopric and returned to evangelistic work among the Frisians, among whom he had begun his missionary career. One day as he prepared to confirm a group of new converts, Boniface and his companions were attacked by a group of pagans. Boniface refused to defend himself and was martyred. Before his death Boniface reported

---

9. Starkes, *God's Commissioned People*, 67.
10. Ibid., 69-70.
11. Neill, *History of Missions*, 75.

that one-hundred-thousand Germans had been baptized through his ministry.[12]

CYRIL AND METHODIUS

Two brothers, Cyril and Methodius, are remembered as the great missionary evangelists among the Slavic people. In about 862 Prince Ratislav of Moravia asked Emperor Michael III of Byzantium to send missionaries to his country. The emperor chose Cyril and Methodius to carry out this mission. They began work in Crimea and later moved into Bulgaria, Bohemia, and Moravia. They prepared the first alphabet of the Slavonic language and translated the Bible, the liturgy, and other religious literature into Slavonic. This material was a great help in their evangelistic work.[13]

Cyril and Methodius used a unique form of evangelism to bring about the conversion of King Bogoris of Bulgaria. Bogoris asked Methodius to paint a scene on the wall of his palace. Methodius painted a graphic picture of the rewards of heaven and the torments of hell. When the painting was unveiled, the king and many of his court officials accepted baptism. King Bogoris also ordered all of his people to accept baptism or be killed.[14]

Through the influence of Cyril and Methodius, Slavonic, rather than Latin, became the official language of the Bulgarian church. They also set the pattern for the churches of eastern Europe. Each nation organized a state church that was independent of Rome and employed its own language and its own leadership. This was very different from the pattern employed by the Roman Catholic Church, which used one language and centralized power under the pope of Rome.[15]

FRANCIS OF ASSISI

Protestants and Catholics alike acknowledge Francis of Assissi (1182-1226) as one of the great evangelists of the later

---

12. Rudnick, *Speaking the Gospel*, 71.
13. Ibid., 65.
14. W. O. Carver, *The Course of Christian Missions* (New York: Fleming H. Revell Co., 1939), 69.
15. Rudnick, *Speaking the Gospel*, 65.

Middle Ages. Francis, the son of a wealthy merchant, spent his youth living as a pampered playboy. When he was twenty-seven, God spoke to him through the words of Jesus: "As you go, preach this message: 'The kingdom of heaven is near.' Heal the sick, raise the dead, cleanse those who have leprosy, drive out demons. Freely you have received, freely give" (Matt. 10:7-8).

This call from God transformed Francis' life. He forsook the luxuries of his former life and devoted himself to serving the poor. He vowed to live in poverty and forsake the pleasures of the world. He began to travel from village to village preaching to the people and rebuilding dilapidated chapels. Soon a group of disciples gathered around Francis. Francis wrote a set of rules for his followers, and the pope gave this new order of friars his official approval. They aimed to comfort the poor and evangelize the heathen. Francis sent them out two-by-two to preach. They went barefooted and lived on the food the people gave them. Francis was especially effective in his evangelistic work for two reasons. First, his life-style of self-sacrifice and simplicity attracted many people. Second, he used music very effectively. He sang to his hearers and moved their hearts.[16]

JOHANN TAULER

One of the great evangelical preachers of the late Middle Ages was Johann Tauler (1300-1361). A disciple of Meister Eckhart, he was influenced by the mystical group, the Friends of God. These mystics believed they could achieve union with God through fasting, prayer, and meditation. Tauler was already a popular and respected pastor in Strasbourg, Alsace, when a friend persuaded him that he needed spiritual enlightenment. In response Tauler left his church and spent two years in prayer, searching for the "higher life." The first time Tauler tried to preach after his spiritual retreat he wept so much he had to stop. After that when he preached, the congregation wept, groaned, and even fainted.

---

16. Roland Q. Leavell, *Evangelism: Christ's ImperativeCommission* (Nashville: Broadman Press, 1979), 67-68.

Tauler became the most powerful preacher of his day. He influenced many people in the towns and villages along the Rhine River. His converts did not leave the Roman Catholic Church. Instead, they formed prayer groups that sought spiritual union with God. Martin Luther said that reading Tauler's sermons in later years affected him deeply.[17]

EVANGELIZATION BY RULERS

Conversion by force was the rule rather than the exception in much of medieval Europe. Actions like that of King Bogoris were quite common.

CHARLEMAGNE

A classic example of forced conversion is Charlemagne's action toward the Saxons. Charlemagne, king of the Franks, was the greatest political leader of the early Middle Ages, ruling much of what is now Germany and France. Charlemagne was dedicated to Christianity (though this did not carry over to his personal morals) and sent out many missionaries to evangelize the various parts of his large kingdom. In 800 Pope Leo III crowned him emperor of the Holy Roman Empire. Charlemagne mounted a military campaign to subdue the Saxon tribes living along the northern border of his kingdom. When he invaded their territory, Charlemagne brought along missionaries, thinking that evangelizing the fierce Saxons would also pacify them. The Saxons proved as hard to evangelize as they were to conquer. Charlemagne had to conduct twenty military campaigns before the Saxons finally surrendered. During his military occupation Charlemagne declared that both refusing to accept baptism and showing disrespect for Christianity were crimes punishable by death. Charlemagne probably had mixed motives for evangelizing the Saxons. Undoubtedly, he believed that they would become more willing and pliable subjects once they had accepted the official religion of his kingdom. On the other hand, Charlemagne

---

17. Ibid., 69-70.

was dedicated to the church and had a sincere desire to see the Saxon people become Christians.[18]

PRINCESS OLGA

Russia became Christian through the efforts of a saintly woman and her powerful grandson. Princess Olga was attracted to Christianity and traveled to Constantinople to learn more about the faith. She was baptized in 955 and returned to Russia hoping to evangelize her son, King Swiatoslav. She failed to win him, but her grandson, Vladimir, proved more responsive. When Vladimir became king, he sent representatives to study Judaism, Islam, Roman Catholicism, and Greek Orthodox Christianity. He finally decided that Greek Orthodoxy the was best religion. In 988 Vladimir proclaimed Christianity the official religion of his kingdom. He destroyed the national idol, had his army baptized en masse, and ordered his subjects to become Christians. He asked the emperor at Constantinople to send missionaries to instruct his people.[19]

Not all efforts at forced conversion were successful. Germanic princes tried to conquer and convert the Wends, a Slavic tribe that lived between the Elbe and Oder rivers along the Baltic seacoast. Although the Wends were defeated militarily, they never did accept Christianity. Finally, the whole tribe was forcibly relocated and replaced by German-speaking people.[20]

INTERPRETATION AND APPLICATION

The concept of evangelism changed dramatically during the Middle Ages. In the church of New Testament times, evangelism was persuading people to accept Jesus Christ as their Savior, while in the Middle Ages evangelism was incorporating people into the church. The evangelists of the Middle Ages thought of evangelism in sacramental terms. They believed that people were saved by means of the church sacraments, especially baptism and

---

18. Rudnick, *Speaking the Gospel*, 59-60.
19. Carver, *Christian Missions*, 70.
20. Rudnick, *Speaking the Gospel*, 60.

holy communion. Therefore, their primary concern was to persuade people to submit to baptism. The forced conversions discussed above also lowered the level of Christianity practiced in most churches. In many areas Christianity was little more than a thin veneer covering the traditional religion of the people. Often, superstitions played a larger role in the lives of church members than did Christian doctrine and ethics.

WHY DID CHRISTIANITY SPREAD?

1. *Many converted because they were forced to do so.* Many rulers forced their subjects to accept baptism. The rulers were more successful in this than in changing the world view of their people.

2. *Rather primitive peoples were attracted by the more advanced culture of Rome and its former territories.*

3. *Many ancient Europeans found Christianity's answers to the questions of life more appealing than those offered by pagan religions.*

4. *Many converted because they wanted to enter into the delights of heaven and avoid the sufferings of hell.*

5. *Many were impressed with the "enthusiasm and conviction with which the faith was propagated."* Latourette believed this last reason was the primary reason.[21]

HOW DID CHRISTIANITY SPREAD?

1. *Christianity expanded along its frontier.* Christianity was spread primarily by groups of people who had become Christians recently. New converts seem to have been more motivated to share their newfound faith.

2. *The Roman popes dedicated the resources of the church to evangelizing Europe.*

---

21. Kenneth S. Latourette, *A History of the Expansion of Christianity*, 7 vols. (New York: Harper & Row, 1938), 2:146.

3. *Monasticism was an important evangelizing force, especially in the early Middle Ages.* Later, mendicant orders like the Franciscans and Dominicans were effective.

4. *Most conversions occurred in large groups.* These group movements, sometimes called mass movements, were usually engineered by the group's leader. Occasionally, the rulers used force to assure compliance with their decision. Some kings decreed conversion because of their religious convictions, but in other cases the kings ordered the people to become Christians in order to disarm potential rivals who clung to the old religion.[22]

LESSONS FOR US

The Middle Ages teach modern evangelists two important lessons:

1. *Dedicated individuals can make a great difference.* Boniface and Francis had few resources, but they accomplished great things for God.

2. *Sharing the gospel with rulers is important.* Government leaders have the capacity to influence vast numbers of people.

STUDY QUESTIONS

1. What was the major force in evangelism in the Middle Ages?

2. How did monasteries evangelize an area?

3. Who were three of the great missionary evangelists of this era?

4. What role did Charlemagne play in Christianizing Europe?

---

22. Ibid., 2:144-46.

— 5 —

FORERUNNERS OF THE REFORMATION

Devout Christians prepared the kindling for the fires of reformation long before Martin Luther challenged the Roman Catholic Church. Evangelism in the Middle Ages consisted primarily of persuading people to accept baptism. The Roman Catholic Church taught that baptism brought a person into the church, which alone could dispense salvation. The priests taught that salvation came through baptism and the mass. Sometimes popes intimidated kings and kingdoms by withholding these sacraments or threatening to do so. By the use of this power Pope Gregory VII (1073-85) forced Emperor Henry IV to kneel in the snow for three days begging forgiveness from the pope.

Church worship was characterized by great formality and pomp. However, the Scriptures had little importance. Many priests could barely read. The people knew very little of the Scriptures because the Bible was only available in Latin, a language few common people understood.

During the later Middle Ages the Roman Church became increasingly corrupt. Some of the popes lived openly with their mistresses and fathered illegitimate children. Church officials bought and sold church positions, and many sought high positions solely to enrich themselves. Many parish priests lacked education and gave little time to their pastoral duties. Drunkenness and immorality among priests were common rather than the exception. The common people lived miserably, in bondage to superstition and fear. Still, in those dark days God lit several candles.

PETER WALDO AND THE WALDENSES

One group that evangelized actively during this period was the Waldenses. Primarily known as a dissenting group that broke with the Roman Catholic Church, they are also notable for their evangelism.

Peter Waldo, a wealthy merchant from Lyons in southern France, founded the group. In 1170 Peter had a profound religious experience and committed himself to a life of poverty and preaching. He resolved to live by Jesus' words in Matthew 19:21: "If you want to be perfect, go, sell your possessions and give to the poor, and you will have treasure in heaven. Then come, follow me." Waldo obeyed this command literally. He sold his possessions, made provision for his wife and children, and gave the rest of his money to the poor.[1]

RISE OF THE WALDENSES

Freed from financial concerns, Peter traveled throughout southern France preaching in the towns and villages. Like Francis of Assisi, he took nothing with him, living on what the villagers gave him. His simple life-style stood in stark contrast to the luxury enjoyed by the hierarchy of the Roman Church. As you might expect, the bishops did not appreciate the comparison.

Peter soon gained popularity and a wide following in southern France. He preached powerful sermons and quoted long passages of the New Testament from memory. This type of preaching really appealed to the common people, who rarely heard the Bible in Latin, much less in their own language. Peter soon attracted a group of followers who called themselves the Poor Men of Lyons. They copied Peter Waldo's simple life-style and devoted themselves to lay preaching and memorizing the Bible.

---

1. M. Thomas Starkes, *God's Commissioned People* (Nashville: Broadman, 1984), 96.

In the beginning Peter and his followers had no thought of breaking with the Roman Church. Peter just wanted to preach the gospel to the poor. He went to Rome during the Third Lateran Council to request recognition for his group. Pope Alexander III granted the Poor Men limited authority to preach but warned them to ask permission from the local priests and bishops first. Peter and his Poor Men agreed to do this, but the priests of Lyons denied their request to preach publicly. Peter declared, "We ought to obey God rather than men," and his followers continued to preach. As a result, the Council of Verona excommunicated them in 1184. The excommunication apparently did not slow their growth because the Waldenses spread into Italy, Germany, Bohemia, Spain, and the Netherlands. The Catholic hierarchy persecuted them aggressively and even mounted a crusade against them in southern France. During this time many Waldenses fled to isolated valleys in the Alps, where they took refuge. Many later joined the Reformed Church or the Anabaptists, but some remained distinct. A Waldensian Church still exists today in Europe, Uruguay, and North Carolina.

TEACHINGS OF THE WALDENSES

The Waldenses emphasized the Bible in their preaching and teaching. Peter sponsored translations of the Bible in local languages, and he encouraged his followers to memorize the Scriptures and live by them. The Waldenses stressed the importance of preaching, and they allowed both laymen and laywomen to preach. They taught that Christians should live according to the Sermon on the Mount. They rejected masses and prayers for the dead and preached that purgatory is simply the troubles that affect Christians in their earthly lives. They rebelled against worshiping in Latin because the common people could not understand it. They declared that sacraments offered by immoral priests were invalid and taught that laymen could hear confession. They refused to take oaths and held that any taking of human life is sin. Eventually, they ordained their own clergy and had bishops, priests, and deacons to lead their church.[2]

---

2. Kenneth Scott Latourette, *A History of Christianity* (New York: Harper & Row, 1953), 452-53.

The Waldenses attracted favorable attention by their way of living. Latourette described them in this way:

For the most part the Waldenses were humble folk. Even their enemies described them as dressing simply, industrious, laboring with their hands, chaste, temperate in eating and drinking, refusing to frequent taverns and dances, sober and truthful in speech, avoiding anger, and regarding the accumulation of wealth as evil.[3]

IMPORTANCE OF THE WALDENSES

As evangelists the Waldenses were noted for several things:

1. *The Waldenses preached to anyone who would listen.* They dispatched missionary pairs to establish new congregations across Europe.

2. *The Waldenses emphasized the Bible.* They centered everything on the Scriptures.

3. *The Waldenses preached to the people in the local language.* Refusing to use Latin, they made the gospel clearly understandable to all.

4. *The Waldenses' simple life-style attracted many people and proved their sincerity and dedication.*

5. *The Waldenses influenced later reforming groups.* They influenced the Hussites, Taborites, and through them the Bohemian Brethren. Some evidence indicates that they had some influence on the Lollards and on the Anabaptists. Certainly, they helped condition Europe for the Protestant Reformation.

JOHN WYCLIFFE AND THE LOLLARDS

Several historians have called John Wycliffe (1329-1384) the "Morning Star of the Reformation." By this they mean that

---

3. Ibid.

John Wycliffe's deeds and writings signaled the coming of the Reformation.[4]

Wycliffe's early years certainly revealed no inclination on his part to stir up controversy. Instead, he spent most of his life as a student and professor at Oxford University in England. In fact, Wycliffe once admitted that Oxford was his one true love. He lived quietly at the university and slowly built a reputation as one of the leading philosophers and theologians of his time. He did not begin agitating for reform in the church until the last eight or nine years of his life.[5]

Motives for Wycliffe's Reforms

Several factors motivated Wycliffe to take up the cause of church reform:

1. *Wycliffe opposed church wealth.* In 1373 he travelled to the court of the pope in Avignon, France. The luxury and corruption he observed there offended him deeply. He also reacted negatively to the accumulation of wealth by the monasteries in England. He could not reconcile the affluent life-styles of the church hierarchy with the poverty of the peasants.

2. *Wycliffe opposed the abuse of political power by the church.* The papal schism (a time when there were two popes) troubled him. He questioned whether Christians should acknowledge the authority of church officials who abused their positions.

3. *Wycliffe wanted the common people to have pastoral care.* Many parishes were served by absentee priests who received a salary but did not live in the town or serve the people. This lack of pastoral care and the low level of literacy caused most of the people to be dominated by superstition.

4. G. H. W. Parker, *The Morning Star: Wycliffe and the Dawn of the Reformation* (Grand Rapids: Eerdmans Publishing Co., 1965), 56.
   5. Ibid., 22.

4. *Wycliffe was an English nationalist.* During his later years the kings of France, with whom the English were at war, controlled the popes in Avignon. Wycliffe and many other Englishmen resented the money that the English turned over to the pope's treasury.

In his later years Wycliffe's theology grew increasingly radical. The officials of the Roman Church noticed this, and the pope condemned Wycliffe's views in 1377. However, these church officials could not prosecute Wycliffe because he had friends among the English nobility. John of Gaunt, the Duke of Lancaster, protected Wycliffe from physical harm, though he could not shield Wycliffe from all censure.[6]

WYCLIFFE AND THE BIBLE

Wycliffe based his theology on the authority of the Bible. This was a radical concept in his time. He insisted that the Bible has authority superior to that of the pope or a church council. He expressed his views on the Bible most clearly in his 1378 work, *On the Truth of Holy Scripture.* His main thesis was simple. He wrote that the Bible was the highest authority for every believer, the measure of correct doctrine, and the guide for reform of church, state, and person. Wycliffe believed all the Scriptures were inspired by God and were completely sufficient to lead a person to salvation. This last concept directly contradicted Roman Catholic doctrine. In Wycliffe's time the Roman Church taught that salvation could be had only through the church which dispensed it to those who were faithful and cooperative.[7]

Wycliffe also moved a long way toward the doctrine of the priesthood of all believers. His view was not the fully developed doctrine as taught by Luther and Calvin later, but he did teach that anyone could understand the Bible if they had faith and the help of the Holy Spirit. This, too, was contrary to the teachings of the church that held that only priests could interpret the Bible.[8]

---

6. Tim Dowley, *Eerdmans' Handbook to the History of Christianity* (Grand Rapids: Eerdmans Publishing Co., 1977), 338.

7. Parker, *Morning Star,* 43.

8. Ibid.

Wycliffe's devotion to biblical authority led him to challenge other church practices as well. He rejected transubstantiation, the belief that the bread and wine actually become the body and blood of Christ during the mass. He rejected the infallibility and ultimate authority of the pope and said that Christ was head of the church. He also protested the sale of indulgences, certificates of forgiveness sold to people who wished to reduce their time of suffering in purgatory.

THE LOLLARDS

To propagate his views and minister to the needs of the English people, Wycliffe wrote a number of treatises. Many of these were meant for academic audiences in the universities of Europe, but he wrote others for the common people. His concern for the spiritual welfare of the common people prompted Wycliffe to direct the translation of the Bible into English and appoint a number of "Poor Priests," who served as traveling evangelists. The Poor Priests were one of Wycliffe's greatest contributions. Wycliffe believed that laymen could and should be trained to preach the gospel. He argued that the common people needed to hear the gospel in their own language. Wycliffe held a high view of preaching, saying it was "a holier act than the consecration of the sacrament." Wycliffe declared that the primary duties of a priest were to set a moral example for his people and to preach the gospel.[9]

Perhaps the example of Francis of Assisi and his followers inspired Wycliffe to send out his Poor Priests. Like Francis, Wycliffe encouraged his men to preach wherever they could gather a crowd—on the road, in churches, and on village greens. He instructed them to wear long russet-colored robes and sandals. They carried long staffs but no purses. They accepted whatever food and shelter was offered them but did not ask for money. They preached in English and shared portions of the Bible in English with the people. Often they repeated sermons taught to them by Wycliffe, who emphasized the exposition of the Bible. In the beginning most of the Poor Priests were young men who had

---

9. Ibid., 47-48.

studied under Wycliffe at Oxford University, but in later years most were poor, unlearned men. Also, many of the first group were ordained priests, but later Wycliffe sent out laymen. Wycliffe defended their ministry, saying a divine call was more important than church ordination.[10]

Wycliffe did not mean to establish a new order of traveling monks, nor did he want to challenge the parish priests. He just wanted to make sure that the common people heard the gospel. He encouraged his Poor Priests to take the "bare text of Scripture" and explain it to the people. Wycliffe himself set a good example in this. His surviving sermons are careful expositions of Scripture that point people to Christ. Wycliffe was convinced that the Bible should be the rule of life, and he imparted this truth to his traveling evangelists.[11]

Wycliffe's preachers soon gained a large number of disciples who came to be called "Lollards." This term came from a word meaning "to mumble." It referred to their practice of reciting Bible verses and saying prayers. The Lollards accepted Wycliffe's theology and believed in the authority of the Bible, worship in English, and the independence of the laity. The number of Lollards grew rapidly, at least until the Roman Church began to persecute them. In fact, one historian of Wycliffe's time wrote: "They were everywhere. A man could scarcely meet two people on the road but one of them was a disciple of Wycliffe." No doubt, this was an exaggeration, but it does reflect the popularity of Wycliffe's movement.[12]

Wycliffe's views, especially those on transubstantiation and church authority, so angered the bishops that they forced Wycliffe to leave his beloved Oxford. He went to Lutterworth, where he had been pastor for several years, and devoted himself to writing, preaching, and training his Poor Priests. He also used the time to supervise his Oxford students as they translated the Latin Bible into English. He died peacefully in 1384.[13]

---

10. Latourette, *History of Christianity*, 664-65.

11. Parker, *Morning Star*, 50.

12. Ibid. See also "The Lollards" in *Christian History*, Vol. II, No. 2, Issue 3, 17.

13. Dowley, *Eerdmans' Handbook*, 338.

After Wycliffe's death the Roman Church began to persecute the Lollards aggressively. They could not touch Wycliffe himself, but in 1415 the Council of Constance condemned both Wycliffe and his writings. They ordered his bones exhumed and burned. They may have burned his bones, but his ideas lived on.

WYCLIFFE'S CONTRIBUTIONS TO EVANGELISM

Wycliffe's made various contributions to Christianity, and his influence and the influence of his writings carried forward into the Protestant Reformation. Three of his contributions are of great importance for evangelism:

1. *Wycliffe, like Peter Waldo, emphasized the importance of the Bible.* He encouraged Bible translation, proclamation, memorization, and application to daily life.

2. *Wycliffe emphasized the importance of the laity in church life.* He believed they could interpret the Bible for themselves as well as teach it and preach it.

3. *Wycliffe wanted all people to hear the good news of salvation in English rather than Latin.* He taught that salvation comes through hearing and believing God's Word.

Truly, he was the Morning Star of the Reformation.

JAN HUS AND THE HUSSITES

Jan Hus (1369-1415) was a native of Bohemia in what is now Czechoslovakia. He was a student, then a professor, and finally dean of the University of Prague. In 1402 he became the regular preacher at Bethlehem Chapel in Prague, a chapel where reform of the church was a popular topic. Because of his new preaching duties, Hus began a careful study of the Scriptures. This study led him to question many church practices.

INFLUENCES ON HUS

Several factors combined to shape the situation in Prague during Hus's time.

1. *Several Bohemians who studied at Oxford brought Wycliffe's writings to Prague.* Hus found that he agreed with Wycliffe on several points, especially the authority of Scripture and the need to reform the church.

2. *Germans dominated the university and the church in Bohemia.* Hus was swept up in a rising tide of Bohemian nationalism and resentment against German influence.

3. *Corruption in the Roman Catholic Church frustrated Hus and many of his colleagues.*

4. *The Waldenses had attracted a large number of converts in Bohemia, especially among the common people.* This reformist group was probably familiar to Hus.[14]

HUS'S WITNESS

Like Wycliffe, Hus stressed the authority of Scripture and its role in the Christian's daily life. He encouraged his parishioners and students to live lives of piety and purity. He made preaching an important part of the worship service. He rejected the idea that priests can forgive sins and objected to the sale of indulgences. Hus held that the pope did not have the authority to establish a doctrine that was unscriptural. He criticized the worship of images in the church and religious pilgrimages. He believed that the laity should receive the cup during communion. Hus's main concern was to eliminate corruption in the church and to encourage spiritual reform.[15]

Hus's personal piety and charisma made him a popular figure in Prague. At times he served as the queen's personal chap-

---

14. Parker, *Morning Star,* 74.
15. Dowley, *Eerdmans' Handbook,* 330.

lain, and large crowds came to hear him preach. In 1409 he offended the German faction at the university by defending the views of Wycliffe and condemning corrupt clergy. They retaliated by complaining to the bishop of Prague, who was also a German. In 1410 Hus was excommunicated from the Catholic Church and forced to leave the university. He left Prague, but he continued to preach in the countryside. He attracted many followers there through his preaching in the local language.

In 1414 the Council of Constance ordered Hus to appear and explain his views. He resisted the summons, fearing for his life. However, when Emperor Sigismund gave Hus a guarantee of safe conduct, he felt safe enough to go. When Hus arrived at Constance, he was imprisoned. He appeared before the council, but he did not have an opportunity to express completely his beliefs. The council branded him a Wycliffite and ordered his execution. For political reasons Sigismund refused to intervene, and in 1415 Jan Hus was burned at the stake. He died singing a hymn of praise to Jesus Christ.

HUS'S FOLLOWERS

After Hus's execution his followers divided into two groups: the mainly aristocratic Utraquists and the Taborites who gained followers from the poorer classes. The Utraquists believed in giving both the communion bread and wine to the laity, the unfettered preaching of the gospel, and strict morality on the part of the clergy. They rejected only those practices expressly forbidden by the Bible. The Taborites held similar views, but they took a stricter approach and rejected everything not clearly taught in the Bible. Both groups were persecuted by the pope who sent armies to crush them. From the survivors of these wars came the Bohemian Brethren. Eventually the Brethren migrated to Germany where they became known as the Moravians.[16]

HUS'S SIGNIFICANCE FOR EVANGELISM

Jan Hus is important in the history of evangelism for three reasons:

---

16. Latourette, *History of Christianity*, 669.

1. *Hus emphasized preaching.* His effective expository preaching set an example for others to follow.

2. *Hus insisted on preaching in the language of the people.* He wanted everyone to hear and understand the words and meaning of the Scriptures.

3. *Hus promoted the singing of hymns and spiritual songs.* Congregational singing was an innovation in his time. Choirs provided most music in Catholic services.

Hus's movement influenced the Reformation by its success. As Parker writes: "The significance of the Hussite revolt lay rather in the fact that for the first time the authoritarian claims of the Roman Church had been challenged successfully—in the name of religious reform."[17]

INTERPRETATION AND APPLICATION

The careful reader can easily see that the movements of Waldo, Wycliffe, and Hus have four common concerns:

1. The importance of the Bible in Christian life and worship.

2. Spiritual welfare of the common people.

3. The importance on preaching, rather than sacramentalism.

4. Communication of the gospel in the language of the people.

These three concerns should also be our concerns. Churches today should emphasize the Bible and make it the focus of their preaching and teaching. Churches should not just be "Bible believing"; they should also be Bible preaching. Second, as many denominations become more affluent, more middle-class, there is a danger that churches unintentionally may exclude poor people. These movements of the late Middle Ages set a good example by deliber-

17. Parker, *Morning Star,* 89.

ately targeting the economically disadvantaged. Third, these movements made every effort to communicate in the language of their hearers. This should inspire churches today to provide gospel preaching and teaching in the languages used in their community. Everyone should be able to hear the good news of salvation in their heart language. The example these groups set should also motivate modern witnesses to communicate the message of salvation in terms that the average person can understand. Too often church jargon clouds the gospel rather than clarifies it.

STUDY QUESTIONS

1. What problems in the Roman Catholic Church prompted the development of dissenting groups?

2. Why did the Waldensians translate the Bible into local languages?

3. Why did John Wycliffe send out the Lollards?

4. What was distinctive about the preaching of Jan Hus?

5. What four things did these dissenting groups have in common?

~6~

Evangelism During the Reformation

On October 31, 1517, Martin Luther nailed his Ninety-five Theses to the door of the Wittenberg church. Many historians point to that day as the beginning of the Protestant Reformation. Certainly, that spark touched off the Reformation, but many factors combined to prepare Europe for the Reformation.

What Caused the Reformation?

Political Factors

The Reformation began in Germany. In Luther's time Germany was not a unified nation; rather, it was a collection of small kingdoms ruled by princes. Charles V was the Holy Roman Emperor, in name at least, the sovereign of all the princes. Charles was a loyal Catholic, and he would have thwarted the Reformation had he not been distracted by other problems. At the beginning of the Reformation Charles was preoccupied with wars with France and an invading army from Turkey. Charles was so busy supervising his armies that he had little time for religious controversies.

Social and Economic Factors

At the time of the Reformation civil unrest plagued Germany. This was caused by natural disasters and changes in Germany's economy. Thirteen consecutive years of crop failure brought great suffering to the German people. Also, during this period the German economy was shifting from feudalism toward a modern industrial system. As a result, many farm families left the land to work in mines and new industries in the cities. These social and economic changes left the people open to religious change as well.

INTELLECTUAL FACTORS

The Renaissance helped people to think in new ways and accept new ideas. Also, Erasmus's recently published Greek New Testament inspired many to study the New Testament carefully. The development of European universities and secondary schools raised the intellectual level of the continent. As learning increased, many people abandoned the superstitions that had bound them.

TECHNOLOGICAL FACTORS

The invention of the printing press had a tremendous impact on the Reformation. Presses all over Europe poured out books and pamphlets at a remarkable rate. As William Estep observed, "Without the printing press it would have been difficult, if not impossible, for the Reformation to have crystallized into a highly articulate movement."[1]

RELIGIOUS FACTORS

The people of northern Europe were especially receptive to the Reformation because of widespread corruption in the church. Many of the princes resented the heavy taxes the church placed upon their people. They were particularly upset that the money went to Rome to finance the papal court. Dissenting groups like the Waldenses and Lollards paved the way for the reformers just as John the Baptist prepared the way for Jesus.

---

1. William R. Estep, *The Anabaptist Story* (Grand Rapids: Eerdmans Publishing Co., 1975), 9.

PERSONAL FACTORS

The Reformation progressed in part because of the outstanding leaders involved. Martin Luther, Ulrich Zwingli, and John Calvin were all good scholars, great preachers, and men of faith. Their deeply held convictions motivated them to push the church toward a more biblical Christianity.

EVANGELISM BY THE LUTHERAN CHURCH

When Martin Luther (1483-1546) posted the Ninety-five Theses, he had no idea of starting a religious revolution. He only wanted to protest the sale of indulgences near Wittenberg. The Ninety-five Theses were actually a call for a scholarly debate on the validity of indulgences and the propriety of their sale by the church. However, Luther's theses were printed and distributed all over Europe. Within weeks this obscure professor found himself in the center of a raging controversy.

Luther's public stand against indulgences reflected a long spiritual pilgrimage. Luther was born and raised in northern Germany. At his father's urging he studied law at the University of Erfurt. However, in 1505 Martin was caught in the open by a violent thunderstorm. Afraid for his life, Martin promised God to enter a monastery if his life was spared. Soon after, he joined the Augustinian order. Luther became a dedicated monk and tried to win God's favor by fasting, praying, and depriving his body. He worried constantly about the gravity of his sins. Finally, his superiors assigned him to teach at the new university at Wittenberg, hoping to distract him from his spiritual worry and despair.[2]

At Wittenberg Luther earned a doctorate in theology and became professor of biblical studies. As he prepared his lectures on the Psalms and the Epistles of Paul, he became convinced that human works could never merit salvation. One day while meditating on the meaning of Romans 1:17, Luther understood that salvation comes only through faith. Thus the doctrine of justification by faith became the cornerstone of Luther's theology. This

---

2. Tim Dowley, *Eerdmans' Handbook to the History of Christianity* (Grand Rapids: Eerdmans Publishing Co., 1977), 362-63.

newfound conviction prompted him to oppose the sale of indulgences, certificates of forgiveness sold by the church to raise money.[3] He refused to be silenced. As time passed his views became more extreme, and he denied the supremacy of the pope and the authority of church councils.

In 1521 the pope excommunicated Luther and declared him a heretic. The church would have burned Luther at the stake, but Prince Frederick of Saxony protected him. Eventually, Luther and his loyal colleague, Philip Melancthon, led in establishing what we call the Lutheran Church. This was not their original intent. They meant to reform the Roman Church; but when the hierarchy resisted change, Luther and his disciples felt compelled to establish a church on more biblical grounds.[4] Martin Luther spread the gospel of justification by faith by various means. His message fell upon many receptive ears because the people of Europe were hungry for biblical food.

LUTHER'S TEACHING

Luther continued to teach at the University of Wittenberg even after his excommunication. His convincing arguments from the Scriptures persuaded both faculty and students. Between 1520 and 1560 approximately 16,000 students attended the university; two-thirds of these were from places other than northern Germany. These students carried Luther's evangelical message all over Europe and in turn influenced their own students.[5]

LUTHER'S PREACHING

From 1515 until his death in 1546, Luther preached in the town church of Wittenberg. Through his spoken and printed sermons Luther communicated the gospel to the common people. For Luther, "the preaching of the Word was not just biblical exposition; it was the proclamation of the gospel. Indeed, for Luther any preaching that did not enunciate the gospel of

---

3. Ibid.
4. Ibid.
5. Milton L. Rudnick, *Speaking the Gospel Through the Ages* (St. Louis: Concordia Publishing House, 1984), 81.

redemption was not preaching." Luther did much to restore preaching to its apostolic place of importance in worship and evangelism. He made the preaching of the Word the focus of the worship service.[6]

LUTHER'S WRITINGS

Luther wrote one hundred books and pamphlets to explain his views and spread the gospel. He took full advantage of the new technology—printing. He was one of the first to understand the ability of the printed word to sway the masses.

LUTHER'S BIBLE TRANSLATION

While in hiding at Wartburg Castle, Luther used the time wisely and began translating the New Testament into German. He finished the New Testament in 1522 and the complete Bible in 1534. He revised his work periodically until 1545. Luther's translation became the accepted Bible in German. Luther's work set the standard for German prose for years. However, Luther's purpose for translating was not literary but evangelistic. He wanted to put God's Word into the language of the people so that anyone could read it and find redemption.[7]

LUTHER'S MUSIC

Martin Luther was an enthusiastic musician who sang and played the flute. During his college days he earned spending money performing as a street musician. When he began to reform the church's worship, Luther made congregational hymn singing an important part of the service. He wrote several hymns for this purpose, including the magnificent "A Mighty Fortress Is Our God." Luther understood that the gospel message could be effectively taught through hymns.

6. William R. Estep, *Renaissance and Reformation* (Grand Rapids: Eerdmans Publishing Co., 1986), 155.
7. Dowley, *Eerdmans' Handbook*, 368.

THE SPREAD OF LUTHERANISM

The teachings of Luther spread all over Europe, and the Lutheran Church became the primary church in several northern countries. Luther's students and Lutheran merchants brought the message to the Scandinavian countries. Many people accepted Luther's doctrinal position, but Lutheranism was best established where the rulers adopted it as the state religion. This was true in northern Germany and Scandinavia, but the rulers of eastern and southern Europe opposed his teaching and persecuted budding Lutheran congregations.[8]

European rulers of the sixteenth century had no interest in religious freedom. Their motto was "one faith, one king, and one law." Even where a Protestant church was established, only that denomination was accepted. Generally, the ruler of each principality determined the religion of his subjects. No competition was allowed, but dissenters were allowed to emigrate to other areas where their particular faith was legal.[9] Finland is a good example of how Lutheranism spread. Lutheranism came to Finland and Sweden some time after 1520. Michael Agricola, a Swede who studied under Luther, brought the gospel to Finland. Agricola had to teach the people to read so they could read the Bible he translated for them. By means of his preaching and writing he won Finland to Christ.[10]

LUTHER'S CONTRIBUTIONS TO EVANGELISM

Martin Luther made several important contributions to the cause of evangelism:

1. *Luther's emphasis on justification by faith brought a return to biblical evangelism.* He moved the church away from salvation by works to salvation by grace.

2. *Luther stressed the authority of the Bible.* All true evangelism is based on the authority of the Bible.

---

8. Rudnick, *Speaking the Gospel,* 86.

9. Roland Bainton, *The Reformation of the Sixteenth Century* (Boston: Beacon Press, 1952), 141-42.

10. Ibid., 158-59.

3. *Luther restored preaching to its place of honor in evangelism and worship.*

4. *Luther helped develop church music.* He knew that music could be a real force in evangelism, discipleship, and worship.

5. *Luther taught the priesthood of the believer.* He held that each believer could pray directly to God and understand the Bible through personal study. This was important for evangelism because it restored the element of personal choice.[11]

EVANGELISM BY THE REFORMED CHURCH

Two leaders and their followers combined to establish the Reformed Church.

ZWINGLI'S REFORM

Ulrich Zwingli (1484-1531) was the first of these. Zwingli was born into a middle class family in Switzerland and received a good education at the University of Basel. He studied under the great humanist scholar, Thomas Wyttenbach. Zwingli said that Wyttenbach taught him the sole authority of the Scriptures, the death of Christ as the only price of forgiveness, and the worthlessness of indulgences.

Zwingli became the parish priest at Glarus and soon gained fame as a preacher. In 1519 the great cathedral at Zurich called Zwingli to be the "People's Priest." Zwingli surprised the people of Zurich by preaching expository sermons in German and rejecting the prescribed Latin service. Zwingli also preached against indulgences, priestly celibacy, and fasting during Lent. Some said Zwingli got his ideas from Luther, but Zwingli always maintained that he took his doctrines from the Bible.

Zwingli used preaching, publishing, and public debates to spread his ideas. In 1523 he debated a Catholic scholar in the

---

11. Thomas Starkes, *God's Commissioned People* (Nashville: Broadman Press, 1984), 124.

public plaza of Zurich. In the disputation Zwingli declared that the Bible is the ultimate religious authority, denied the sacrificial nature of the mass, rejected salvation through good works, denied the intercession of the saints, ridiculed the existence of purgatory, and proclaimed the priesthood of all believers. By all accounts Zwingli won the debate, and the city council made a decisive commitment to support church reform.

Zwingli died in a battle against Catholic forces in 1531, but his successor at Zurich, Heinrich Bullinger, carried on his reforming work. Later Zwingli's followers joined with the Calvinists to form the Reformed Church.

CALVIN'S REFORM

John Calvin (1509-1564) was younger than Luther and Zwingli. Born in France in 1509, he was twenty-two years younger than Luther. Some have called him a second generation reformer. Calvin's father wanted him to become a lawyer, but when his father died, Calvin took up the study of theology. In Paris Calvin became acquainted with Luther's writings, and in 1533 he was born again. Forced to leave Paris because of his reformist views, Calvin went to live first in Strassburg and later in Basel, Switzerland.

In 1536 while living in Basel, Calvin published the first edition of his systematic theology, *Institutes of the Christian Religion*. Calvin wrote that Adam's sin was a revolt against the authority of God. Through Adam's sin all humans are corrupted. People are so affected by the fall that they can do nothing to merit their own salvation. Every person deserves the punishment of God, and humanity's only hope is the grace of God. God takes the initiative in salvation. Though God hates sin, He loves the sinner. God loves sinners so much that He sent His own Son to die in their place. Jesus Christ satisfied the righteous judgment of God, removed humanity's curse of sin, and destroyed spiritual death for all who trust in Christ.

Later in 1536 Calvin visited Geneva, and William Farel invited him to assist him in ministry in the city. Calvin agreed, and worked with Farel to establish the Reformation in Geneva. When Calvin took a public stand against immoral practices in the city, the city council forced him to leave Geneva. However, in 1541 he returned to Geneva, and eventually his disciples gained control of the city council. From 1555 until his death in 1564 Calvin exercised virtually a free hand in Geneva.

Many writers have held that Calvin's strong belief in election discouraged him and his followers from doing evangelism. After all, if God has chosen some to be saved, why should Christians interfere in God's work? Some hyper-Calvinists have taken that approach, but Calvin himself did not. Calvin made Geneva the base camp for an intensive evangelistic effort in France. Between 1555 and 1562 Calvin and his colleagues sent eighty-eight evangelists to France. God blessed their efforts because by 1559 the Huguenots (French Calvinists) numbered over one hundred thousand. In 1555 Calvin commissioned a missionary to go to Brazil. All of this reflected Calvin's understanding of the Great Commission. Calvin commented on Matthew 28:19:

> *This is the point of the word go (exeundi): the boundaries of Judea were prescribed to the prophets under the law, but now the wall is pulled down and the Lord orders the ministers of the gospel to go far out to scatter the teaching of salvation throughout all the regions of the earth.*[12]

CALVIN'S CONTRIBUTIONS TO EVANGELISM

1. *Calvin and his followers preached the Bible with boldness.* They challenged their hearers to reject the corrupt doctrines and practices of the Roman Church and receive the pardon, peace, and liberty of the true Gospel.

2. *Calvin and his followers used public debates to popularize their ideas.*

---

12. Timothy George, "The Challenge of Evangelism in the History of the Church," in *Evangelism in the Twenty-First Century,* ed. Thom Rainer (Wheaton, Ill.: Harold Shaw Publishers, 1989), 14; and Estep, *Renaissance and Reformation,* 247.

3. Institutes *was translated into many languages and became the most influential book of the Reformation.* Calvin also published a number of Bible commentaries that revealed his excellent scholarship and guided Reformed pastors in their preaching and teaching.

4. *Calvin made Geneva a model community.* In his last years it became a living laboratory of Christianity.

5. *Calvin and his disciples established the Geneva Academy for training pastors.* Because Geneva became a haven for Protestant refugees from all over Europe, the Academy trained pastors and evangelists who returned to their homelands carrying Calvin's *Institutes* in their hands and his evangelistic concern in their hearts.[13]

One outstanding example of this was John Knox (1514-1572). A native of Scotland, Knox was ordained as a priest in 1536, but soon afterward he became a reformer. Forced to flee Scotland, Knox studied for a time in Geneva. In 1559 he returned to Scotland and became the leader of the Reformation there. He carried on a running feud with Mary Queen of Scots. Knox helped to establish the Presbyterian Church in Scotland by means of his fiery preaching, writings, and especially by the force of his personality.[14]

EVANGELISM BY THE ANABAPTISTS

Though Luther, Calvin, and Zwingli actively spread the gospel, it was the Anabaptists who most actively evangelized sixteenth-century Europe. The three principal reformers wanted to reform the church, but the Anabaptists wanted to revolutionize the church and restore it to New Testament purity. This course

---

13. Rudnick, *Speaking the Gospel*, 88-89; and Estep, *Renaissance and Reformation*, 246.

14. John Knox, *Wycliffe Biographical Dictionary of the Church* (Chicago: Moody Press, 1982), 230.

brought them into conflict with both Catholics and Protestants, and both persecuted the Anabaptists unmercifully.[15]

ANABAPTIST BEGINNINGS

The Anabaptists originated in Zurich, Switzerland. The first Anabaptists were all followers of Ulrich Zwingli, but they split with him over the doctrine of infant baptism and other matters. Several of Zwingli's younger supporters, including Felix Manz, George Blaurock, and Conrad Grebel, wanted to do away with any church practice not explicitly taught in the Scriptures. Zwingli, on the other hand, decided to compromise with the city council so as to retain their support.

On January 21, 1525, a group of people went to the home of Felix Manz. Conrad Grebel baptized George Blaurock, and Blaurock baptized all the others in attendance. In this way the first congregation of the Swiss Brethren was established. Their opponents called them Anabaptists (re-baptizers) because they insisted that the Bible taught believer's baptism rather than infant baptism.[16]

As their group increased, Zwingli and the city council became alarmed and began to persecute them. The authorities imprisoned Grebel and Manz in 1526, and Manz was executed by drowning in 1527. Despite the persecution, Anabaptist congregations were established all over Europe. In fact, the authorities unwittingly aided the spread of Anabaptism by persecuting them. When officials scattered the members of one congregation, the scattered members started other congregations in their new locations much like the Christians from Jerusalem mentioned in Acts 8.[17]

ANABAPTIST TEACHINGS

The Anabaptists were never a unified group. The heavy persecution they suffered kept them fragmented. Still, it is possible to identify some common beliefs. These were expressed in the

---

15. George, "Evangelism in the History of the Church," 15.
16. Estep, *The Anabaptist Story*, 10.
17. Starkes, *God's Commissioned People*, 130.

Schleitheim Confession adopted in 1527. This confession of faith had seven major points:

- Baptism for mature persons who had made a profession of faith;

- Banning from the Lord's Supper those who were living immorally;

- Only baptized believers were allowed to partake of the Lord's Supper;

- Pastors to lead the faithful;

- Separation from the evil and wickedness of the world;

- Non-participation in war and military service;

- Refusal to take oaths or swear allegiance.[18]

The Anabaptists also took a symbolic view of the Lord's Supper and believed passionately in religious liberty and the separation of church and state. Many of them died for their views, but they continued to evangelize despite persecution and martyrdom.

One of the leading Anabaptist evangelists was Balthasar Hubmaier (1481-1528). He was a trained theologian who had taught at several Catholic universities. In 1525 he accepted Anabaptist views and began to preach and publish pamphlets which he printed on his own press. When he was forced to flee Zurich, Hubmaier went to Moravia, where he evangelized so effectively that he baptized six thousand people in one year. Relentlessly pursued by both the government and the Roman Church, Hubmaier was captured and burned at the stake in 1528 in the public square of Vienna.[19]

INTERPRETATION AND APPLICATION

The Protestant reformers did more than just protest against the sad state of the Roman Catholic Church. They rediscovered

---

18. Ibid.

19. Roland Q. Leavell, *Evangelism: Christ's Imperative Commission* (Nashville: Broadman Press, 1979), 80.

the New Testament doctrine of salvation. The reformers did not intend to start new denominations; rather, they wanted to call the Roman Church back to its origins—the authority of the Bible and salvation through the grace of Christ. The Roman hierarchy resisted that change, but the reformers did lay the foundation for Pietism and the awakenings that followed. Their doctrines and example led to the modern missionary movement of the nineteenth century.[20]

ELEMENTS OF REFORMATION EVANGELISM

There were several key elements to Reformation evangelism:

1. *The reformers emphasized biblical preaching in the language of the people.* Their preaching centered on justification by faith.

2. *The reformers exalted the authority of the Bible.* They taught that the Bible is the ultimate authority that governs church doctrine and practice. They also made every effort to provide the Bible in the language of their people. They encouraged the people to read the Bible for themselves. They pointed to the Scriptures as a sufficient source of knowledge about salvation.

3. *The reformers used the printing press to spread their views.* They understood the power of media to influence people.

4. *The reformers seized the opportunity of their day.* Europe was ripe for reform. No evangelist operates in a vacuum. Circumstances affect the results of any evangelist's ministry. Northern Europe responded positively to the reformers, while Italy and Spain did not. The difference was the attitude of the rulers and the situation of the population.

The reformers' experiences should inform evangelism today. In these days of the "health and wealth gospel" evangelists would

---

20. George, "Evangelism in the History of the Church," 13.

do well to return to the reformers' emphasis on justification by faith. Any evangelism that neglects this emphasis is less than the gospel. Also, modern evangelists should take care to teach and submit to Biblical authority. Every message and every word of witness should be grounded in the Scriptures and completely consistent with their teaching. When the message is soundly based on the Bible, the evangelist can confidently say, "thus saith the Lord." Finally, evangelists ought to use the mass media carefully to spread the good news of salvation. Too many evangelistic programs are so dull that only dedicated Christians will watch them. Evangelists should always examine their message and methods to ensure that they are preaching the right thing in the most effective way. The Lord Jesus demands and deserves nothing less.

STUDY QUESTIONS

1. What factors prepared the way for the Protestant Reformation?

2. What methods did Martin Luther use to evangelize the German people?

3. How did John Calvin's view of election affect his evangelism?

4. How did the beliefs of the Anabaptists differ from those of Luther and Calvin?

5. What were the key elements in the evangelism of the Reformers?

⊰7⊱

Pietism and Evangelism

The Origin of Pietism

German Pietism developed as part of a larger spiritual movement that also affected the Church of England and the Dutch Reformed Church in the seventeenth century. German Pietists reacted against the decline in morality caused by the Thirty Years War (1618-1648), a devastating war that pitted the Protestant princes of Germany against the Catholic princes. This war left much of Germany in ruins.

The Pietists also reacted against the dead orthodoxy of Lutheranism. In the Protestant areas of Germany, the   Lutheran Church was the state church. The government assigned pastors to churches and paid their salaries. As a result, many pastors felt little responsibility for or to their people. Because Lutherans continued to practice infant baptism, church membership became a matter of family heritage and a cultural norm rather than of religious conviction. Most worship services were dull, featuring lengthy sermons focusing on correct doctrine rather than correct living.[1]

Most church historians date the beginning of German Pietism at 1675, the year that Philipp Jakob Spener published his

---

1. Dale W. Brown, *Understanding Pietism* (Grand Rapids: Eerdmans Publishing Co., 1978), 21.

Pia Desideria (Earnest Desires). However, the Pietists movement did not begin instantly. Instead, several movements combined to bring it about. The Pietists accepted the key doctrines of Luther's theology: authority of the Scriptures, justification by faith, and the priesthood of the believer. Pietism was also closely related to English Puritanism. The Puritans emphasized moral earnestness, decentralized church polity, devotion to the Bible, and the practice of piety in daily life. Pietists also drew upon the mystical writings of Meister Eckhart, Johann Tauler, Kasper Schwenkfeld, and others. The Anabaptists influenced the Pietists by stressing the new birth, the guidance of the Holy Spirit, and the restoration of primitive Christianity.[2]

THE CHARACTERISTICS OF PIETISM

Lewis Drummond has explained that the most important element in Pietism was religion of the heart. The Pietists insisted that true religion was heartfelt, not just intellectual. The Pietists believed the great doctrines of the faith, they insisted that Christians must internalize those doctrines. They did not reject creeds, but they wanted religion to be experienced. As William Ames stated, "Faith is the resting of the heart in God."[3]

The emphases of Pietistic writings and teachings help us understand their movement.

THE NEW BIRTH

Luther rediscovered justification by faith. The Pietists valued that doctrine, but they emphasized regeneration and sanctification.

RELIGIOUS ENTHUSIASM

The Pietists preached experiential religion, but they distrusted those who claimed to have seen visions and received spe-

---

2. Ibid., 17-26.

3. Lewis Drummond, "The Puritan-Pietistic Tradition," *Review and Expositor* (Fall 1980), 484.

cial revelations. They based their faith solidly on the Word of
God.

JOY

The Pietists often spoke of joyous fellowship with Christ.
They believed that an intimate fellowship with Christ produced
joy in living.

SANCTIFICATION

The Pietists taught that the Holy Spirit would minister to
believers to help them become more like Jesus. However, the
Pietists rejected perfectionism. They did not accept the idea that
a Christian could achieve a state of sinless perfection in this
world.

BIBLICISM

The Pietists valued Scripture. They measured every concept
and practice by God's Word. They also believed the laity could
and should interpret the Bible for themselves with the guidance
of the Holy Spirit.

THEOLOGICAL EDUCATION

The Pietists showed great concern about having well-edu-
cated ministers. Their ideal was a minister who had both a full
knowledge of the Bible and a deep, ongoing relationship with
Christ.

MISSIONS AND EVANGELISM

The Pietists revealed an enthusiasm for evangelism that had
been sadly lacking since the time of Luther and Calvin. Count
Nickolaus von Zinzendorf said, "My joy until I die. . . (is) to win
souls for the Lamb."

SOCIAL CONCERN

Many have accepted the mistaken idea that the Pietists were
so heavenly minded that they were of no earthly good. This

notion does a great disservice to the Pietists. In their writings and their practice they showed a heartfelt and practical concern for those in every kind of need. The Pietists had hope for the world. Rather than rejecting the world, they loved the people of the world and sought to alleviate their problems. They believed changed people could change the world for good.

PIETIST LEADERS

The Pietists believed that the momentum of the Protestant Reformation had been lost to doctrinal dogmatics, institutionalism, and polemics (attacks on other denominations). They wanted to recover the spirituality of the New Testament church by teaching the principles of Christian discipleship and the responsibilities of church membership.

The Pietists strove for a distinctively Christian life-style. They insisted that the orthodoxy of the Protestant churches be coupled with orthopraxis (right living). Pietism was definitely a theology of goodness. The Pietists wanted Christians to do right as well as believe right.[4]

The German Lutheran Church in the 1600s was in the "Age of Dead Orthodoxy." The churches emphasized pure doctrine and the observance of the sacraments rather than Christian experience and service. Church leaders expected the laity to play a passive role in the church. Most pastors considered listening to sermons and partaking of communion the sum total of Christian life.

SPENER

A pastor named Philipp Jakob Spener (1635-1705) interrupted this scene. In 1670, while serving as pastor in Frankfurt, Spener organized a group of church members. They gathered in his home twice a week for prayer and Bible study. He called these cottage prayer meetings *Collegia Pietatis*, and those who attended came to be called Pietists. In 1675 Spener published *Pia Desideria*, a booklet setting forth his criticisms of the church and

---

4. Ibid., 485-86, and Brown, *Understanding Pietism*, 27-28.

calling for reform. Spener criticized the unworthy lives of some pastors and the drunkenness and immorality of the laity. He stated his wishes for the church:

- Intensive Bible study both by individual Christians and by groups;

- More lay participation with renewed emphasis on the priesthood of believers;

- More evidence of Christianity in the daily lives of Christians;

- More evangelism through prayer, moral living, loving deeds, and persuasive witness.

Spener believed these desires could be achieved through the establishment of small devotional groups and through a reformation of preaching.[5]

As you might expect, Spener's recommendations received a mixed response. Many laymen welcomed his new approach, but many pastors opposed him. Finally, they forced him to leave Frankfurt, but he was appointed chaplain to the Duke of Saxony at Dresden. His pietistic preaching also caused a furor at Dresden, and he was forced to leave. Spener accepted a call to a church in Berlin, where he exercised great influence. During his years in Berlin he founded the University of Halle, which became a center of Pietism. He also played a role in promoting religious education and foreign missions. Perhaps his greatest achievement was winning August Hermann Francke to Pietism.

FRANKE

August Hermann Francke (1663-1727) was a devout Lutheran and outstanding professor of biblical studies. He met Spener in 1688 and became an enthusiastic Pietist. Forced to leave the University of Leipzig because of his pietistic views, he eventually was called to pastor a church near Halle and also to teach at the new University of Halle. Francke soon became a leader at the

---

5. Dale Brown, "Pietism," *New Dictionary of Theology* (Downers Grove, Ill.: InterVarsity Press, 1988)

university, and he made it the center of Pietism. Francke set a good example in his classroom by praying before and after his classes and by speaking to his students about their salvation. He encouraged his students to study the Bible carefully and to join prayer groups at the university.

Francke had amazing vision and energy. He established a number of institutions to minister to the needs he observed. These included seven-day schools in the town of Halle, a free boarding school for poor children, an academy for the sons of noble families, a teacher's college, a Bible college, a pharmacy, a bookstore, a printing press that published religious literature, a Bible society, an infirmary, and a home for widows and indigent persons. He also made the University of Halle a center for the training of evangelists and missionaries. The most famous of these was Count Nickolaus von Zinzendorf, a leader of the Moravians and a pioneer in the missions movement.

ZINZENDORF

Nickolaus von Zinzendorf was the son of a German nobleman. Raised in a pious Lutheran home, he studied at Halle as a boy and came under Francke's direct influence. At his father's insistence he studied law and became a civil servant in Saxony. When his father died, he used his inheritance to buy an estate called Berthelsdorf, and invited three hundred Hussites from Bohemia to live on his estate. These people built the village of Herrnhut and established a church. Zinzendorf soon became the pastor of the church, and in 1727 he resigned his government position to devote all his time to the Lord's work.

In 1734 the Lutheran Church ordained Zinzendorf, and he planned to make his Moravians a fellowship within the larger Lutheran Church just as Spener had done. However, the Lutheran leaders in Saxony opposed this. Reluctantly, Zinzendorf became the bishop of the Moravian Brethren. This tiny denomination began sending missionaries all over the world, and Zinzendorf made trips to America and England to organize the work. A true Pietist, he devoted his whole life to heart religion and pure living.

THE CONTRIBUTIONS OF PIETISM TO EVANGELISM

PREACHING TO THE HEART

The Pietists reacted against the cold, doctrinal preaching common in the churches of their day. They believed that sermons should appeal to the emotions as well as to the mind. Their preaching called upon people to respond, to make a personal decision in response to the message.[6]

MISSIONS

The Pietists also made an important contribution to the development of Christian missions. Though William Carey is rightly regarded as the father of the modern missions movement, the Pietists, especially the Moravians, were really the first modern missionaries. Gary Sattler writes that Pietism "was a prime mover in sending theologically trained people for the express purpose of evangelizing other peoples in non-Christian cultures." The Moravians established mission stations in North America, Greenland, Labrador, the British West Indies, Central America, and Africa.[7]

Several principles characterized Pietist missions:

1. *Pietists established schools wherever they went.* They believed that Christians should be taught to read so they could read the Bible.

2. Pietists translated and printed the Bible in the language of the people.

3. *Pietists insisted that their missionaries know the language and culture of the people with whom they worked.* Pietist missionaries sometimes wrote lengthy descriptions of their host cultures in order to instruct new missionaries.

---

6. Gary Sattler, "Moving on Many Fronts," *Christian History*, Vol. V, No. 2, 20.

7. Ibid., 22.

4. *Pietists emphasized personal conversion in their preaching and missionary work.* They endeavored to bring people to a personal decision for Christ.

5. *Pietists moved quickly to establish local indigenous churches led by native pastors.* In this they were well ahead of their time. They tried to be sensitive to the feelings and aspirations of the people with whom they worked. For example, Moravian missionaries asked permission from the Indian tribes of North America before they entered their tribal areas to preach the gospel.[8]

CONVERSION AND HOLINESS

The Pietists focused on experiential aspects of Christianity in contrast to the Lutheran emphasis on abstract formulations. These doctrines provided the theological underpinnings for the awakenings and revivals of the eighteenth and nineteenth centuries. Indeed, Theodore Frelinghuysen, the preacher who initiated the Great Awakening in the Middle Colonies of America, was a Pietist from Germany.[9]

Perhaps the most famous convert to Pietism was John Wesley, the founder of the Methodism. He accepted Christ in a Moravian Church in London and made a trip to Germany to visit Zinzendorf's estate. Both Pietism and Methodism emphasized personal conversion, the power of the Holy Spirit, sanctification, and the importance of small groups in Christian discipleship. Pietism lived on in the Methodist Church. John Wesley's first "little society" reflected this influence by its rules:

1. That we will meet together once a week to "confess our faults to one another, and pray one for another, that we may be healed" (James 5:16).

2. That the persons so meeting be divided into several "bands."

---

8. Ibid.
9. Brown, *Understanding Pietism*, 154.

3. That every one in order speak as freely, plainly, and concisely as he can, the real state of his heart.

4. That all the bands have a conference at eight every Wednesday evening, begun and ended with singing and prayer.[10]

The Pietists made an important contribution to the modern church by demonstrating how evangelistic fervor can be coupled with social concern. The Pietists preached personal conversion, and they also demonstrated their concern for the social and physical needs of the world. They were pacesetters in both missions and social ministry. As Dale W. Brown said:

A frequent stereotype of Pietistic Christianity portrays it as almost exclusively preoccupied with inward devotion and private moral scruples. On the contrary, the Pietist milieu resulted in a desire to transform the living conditions of the poor and oppressed, reform the prison system, abolish slavery, break down rigid class distinctions, establish a more democratic polity, initiate educational reforms, establish philanthropic institutions, increase missionary activity, obtain religious liberty, and propose programs for social justice.[11]

The Pietists hoped to change the world by changing individuals. They tried to practice what they preached and persuade others to follow their example. They did not favor legislating morality; their approach was to love their neighbors, win them to Christ, and teach them to care for others. They truly adopted a servant role in society.[12]

---

10. Ibid., 159; and Albert C. Outler, ed., *John Wesley* (New York: Oxford University Press, 1964), 55.

11. Brown, *Understanding Pietism*, 131.

12. Ibid., 148.

INTERPRETATION AND APPLICATION

The Pietists were forerunners of the modern era of the church.

1. *Pietists emphasized personal conversion.*

2. *Pietists emphasized both personal and group devotions.*

3. *Pietists sought social reform.* They prepared the way for the modern missions movement, the great revivals, and the social reforms supported by the Clapham Sect.

4. *Pietists rescued Protestant Christianity from dry formalism and reinjected a much needed emphasis on personal piety.*

5. *Pietists struck a balance between local evangelism and world missions, setting a good example for evangelistic churches today.* They did their best to win people to Christ in their local area, and they also sent missionaries throughout the world. Too often modern churches seem to focus on one or the other, neglecting a balanced biblical approach.

6. *Pietists evangelized using small groups.* Their cottage prayer meetings and Bible study groups represent methods churches should employ today. Many growing churches throughout the world are using small cell groups as ways to win people to Christ and nurture them in their new faith. Churches do well to remember the importance of small groups, whether these are provided through the Sunday School or some more informal way.

7. *Pietists emphasized both evangelism and social ministry.* Properly done, each complements the other. Showing people how much you care about their needs makes them more receptive to the message of salvation. Many evangelicals today are writing about the

94

church's social obligations. Certainly the Pietists presented a model for modern Christians to imitate.[13]

STUDY QUESTIONS

1. What prompted the development of Pietism?

2. What were the theological emphases of Pietism?

3. Who were three key leaders of the Pietistic movement?

4. What approach did Pietism take to social ministry?

5. What were some characteristic methods of the Pietists?

6. What can modern churches learn from the Pietists?

13. See Delos Miles's book, *Evangelism and Social Involvement* (Nashville: Broadman Press, 1986).

⊹8⊹

REVIVAL IN THE BRITISH ISLES

Historians call the revival in the British Isles the Wesleyan revival, or the Evangelical revival. It began with George Whitefield's outdoor preaching at Bristol, England, in 1739 and ended with John Wesley's death in 1791. Before it ended, the revival changed both British history and church history.[1]

Modern readers can hardly imagine the England of Whitefield and Wesley. There were no railroads and only a few stage coaches. Roads were unmarked and unpaved. There were no hotels or restaurants and only a few inns. Rather than help the poor, the government sent them to debtors' prison. Health conditions were terrible, and few houses had running water. The black plague and smallpox were epidemic, and soap was still not commonly used. Infant mortality was high, and few people lived to reach fifty years of age.[2]

The state of the church and public morality were little better. The churches of England and Scotland showed little vitality. Worship in the Anglican church consisted of rituals and formality. The nobles held religion in disdain, and only five or six members of Parliament even attended worship services. The poorer folk showed no interest in Christianity, and most of them knew little of the Bible. Deism, the belief that God created the world but is

---

1. Milton L. Rudnick, *Speaking the Gospel Through the Ages* (St. Louis: Concordia Publishing House, 1984), 133.
2. "Revival and Revolution," *Christian History* 2, No.1, 7.

not personally involved with the present world, dominated the intellectual scene. Low moral standards and a high level of illiteracy combined to make English society a cesspool of degradation for all but a privileged few.[3]

FORERUNNERS OF REVIVAL

Britain seemed destined for revolution and a slide into agnosticism and anarchy, but three movements prepared the way for the British revival and affected Whitefield and Wesley.

PIETISM

The Pietists worked for a return to personal faith and trust in Christ. They ministered primarily on the continent of Europe, but they established a vibrant mission in England as well. Nickolaus Zinzendorf visited England several times, and the small Moravian churches exercised an influence beyond their size. Furthermore, many in England read the literature of Pietism. Susanah Wesley, the mother of John, avidly read Francke's writings.[4]

PURITANISM

The Puritans also affected the British revival. The great Puritan writers of the previous century were still widely read. Most literate families owned a copy of John Bunyan's *Pilgrim's Progress*. Richard Baxter's *A Call to the Unconverted* and *The Saints' Everlasting Rest* continued to influence the lives of English people long after the author's death. The Puritans emphasized the need for repentance and holy living. John Wesley built on their foundation when he taught the necessity of sanctification (the process by which the Holy Spirit makes the believer more and more like Christ).[5]

---

3. Ibid., and Paulus Scharpff, *History of Evangelism* (Grand Rapids: Eerdmans Publishing Co., 1966), 64-65.

4. Scharpff, *History of Evangelism*, 65, and Lewis Drummond, "The Puritan Pietistic Tradition," *Review and Expositor* (Fall 1980), 489.

5. Scharpff, *History of Evangelism*, 65.

REVIVAL IN AMERICA

The Great Awakening, a revival in America, began about ten years earlier than the British revival. Both the American and British revivals descended directly from the Moravian movement, but in both cases the sons grew taller than their father. The emphasis of the Great Awakening on itinerant evangelism and the conversion of church members had a marked impact on the British revival as well. This is not surprising in light of the close connection between the American colonies and their mother country and the constant interchange between England and the colonies.[6]

GEORGE WHITEFIELD AND THE REVIVAL'S BEGINNING

George Whitefield was born in 1714 in Gloucester. The son of a saloon keeper, he attended Oxford University on a work scholarship. While studying at Oxford, Whitefield met John and Charles Wesley in 1733. Charles invited Whitefield to breakfast and introduced him to John, who was already a member of the faculty. Despite the differences in age and social status the three became good friends. Whitefield joined the Holy Club that the Wesleys had organized to encourage students in their devotional lives.[7]

WHITEFIELD'S SPIRITUAL FORMATION

Whitefield committed his life to Christ in 1735, and the next year was ordained as a deacon in the Church of England. Even as a young man, Whitefield was an impressive speaker. He spoke to a number of large meetings in London, Bristol, and Gloucester in 1737. At the invitation of the Wesleys he spent most of 1738

---

6. Ibid., 66.
7. Rudnick, *Speaking the Gospel,* 137, and Tim Dowley, *Eerdmans' Handbook to the History of Christianity* (Grand Rapids: Eerdmans Publishing Co., 1977), 440.

ministering in Georgia. He decided to establish an orphanage in Georgia and returned to England to raise the necessary funds.[8]

In January of 1739 Whitefield was ordained as a minister. His ordination followed just after a profound personal revival. On January 1, 1739, at Fetter Lane in London, Whitefield joined with John and Charles Wesley and a Moravian evangelist named Benjamin Ingham for a prayer meeting. John Wesley described the event this way:

> *About three in the morning as we were continuing instant in prayer, the power of God came mightily upon us insomuch that many cried out for exceeding joy and many fell to the ground. As soon as we were recovered a little from that awe and amazement at the presence of His majesty, we broke out with one voice, "We praise Thee, O God, we acknowledge Thee to be the Lord."[9]*

This extraordinary prayer meeting was the Pentecost that launched the revival.

FIELD PREACHING

This Fetter Lane experience brought about a change in Whitefield's message and his methods. Before, he had preached salvation by grace and works, but after his spiritual Pentecost he preached salvation through grace alone. His style of preaching also changed. Before he was filled with the Spirit, he read all his sermons from manuscript; but after his Fetter Lane experience, Whitefield began preaching extemporaneously. He also began to preach outdoors. Whitefield took to the fields to preach because many pastors closed their churches to him and because few churches could contain the crowds that came to hear the "boy preacher."[10]

---

8. For more information on Whitefield see Arnold A. Dallimore, *George Whitefield* (Carlisle, Pa.: Banner of Truth Trust, 1970).

9. John Wesley, *Wesley's Works*, 3d ed. Vol. 1, (Grand Rapids: Baker Book House, 1991), 170.

10. Rudnick, *Speaking the Gospel*, 135-36.

The breakthrough in Whitefield's evangelistic ministry came in February, 1739, when he went to Kingswood, a coal mining town near Bristol. The miners and their families lived in miserable conditions: no school, no church, and no hope of economic advancement. On a cold Saturday afternoon Whitefield invited the people to leave their shacks and come hear him preach at a field called Rose Green. About two hundred people attended the first meeting. Encouraged, Whitefield announced a second open-air meeting several days later, and more than two thousand attended. Attendance increased steadily until more than twenty thousand gathered for each service. Whitefield rejoiced to see hardened miners weep for joy as tears of repentance streamed down their grimy faces.[11]

When news of the great revival got out, other cities invited Whitefield to preach. He preached in Bristol, Gloucester, and in the public parks of London. In the parks he sometimes preached to crowds as large as forty thousand. The young preacher became the talk of England. However, Whitefield was concerned about the people in the Bristol area and also about his orphans in Georgia. When he finalized plans to return to Georgia, he invited John Wesley to come to Bristol to take over his evangelistic ministry there. Wesley hesitated to accept the invitation because he had reservations about open-air preaching and about his ability to sway the crowds as Whitefield had. However, after attending several of Whitefield's meetings, Wesley agreed to take over. Although he did not attract crowds as large as Whitefield's, the attendance still was good as was the response.

PASSING LEADERSHIP TO WESLEY

In both Bristol and London the younger Whitefield endorsed Wesley and presented him as his successor. This magnanimous gesture on Whitefield's part gave the revival continuity. Though Whitefield gave John Wesley his start as an evangelist, Wesley's abilities and enthusiasm soon brought him to prominence as the leader of the revival.

---

11. Ibid.

Whitefield, for his part, went back to America, where he founded his orphanage and made a preaching tour of the colonies that was a highlight of the Great Awakening.[12]

In retrospect, Whitefield was the pioneer of the revival. His meetings in Bristol and London signaled the beginning of the public phase of the revival. He was the first to preach outdoors and the first to itinerate. He also was the bridge between the revivals in England, Scotland, and America. Truly George Whitefield was a key figure in the history of evangelism as well as the history of preaching.[13]

JOHN WESLEY AND THE METHODISTS

John Wesley was born in 1703 in the Anglican vicarage at Epworth, where his father served as pastor. After studying at home with his devout mother, Susannah, John entered the Charterhouse School in London and later enrolled at Oxford University. He excelled in his studies and earned bachelor's and master's degrees at Oxford. One of his favorite books was William Law's *Serious Call to a Devout and Holy Life*. He became a lecturer in Greek at Oxford, and in 1726 he was ordained a deacon. After serving for two years as his father's assistant, John returned to Oxford, where he was ordained as a priest by the Church of England. At that time his brother Charles, a student at Oxford, organized a group called the "Holy Club." John assumed leadership of the group and encouraged the members to give themselves to prayer, meditation, and worship. Worldly students dubbed them "Methodists" because of their methodical approach to Christian piety.[14]

In 1735 John and Charles accepted an invitation to go to Georgia as chaplains in General Oglethorpe's new colony. A group of Moravians boarded the same ship, and their calm during a violent storm at sea deeply impressed John. In Georgia John met a

---

12. Ibid.

13. Dowley, *Eerdmans' Handbook*, 446.

14. Thomas Starkes, *God's Commissioned People* (Nashville: Broadman, 1984), 146. A readable biography of John Wesley is John Pollock, *John Wesley* (Wheaton, Ill.: Victor Books, 1989).

Moravian missionary named Spangenberg who asked him disturbing questions about his spiritual condition. Both John and Charles had unpleasant experiences in Georgia. Charles did not get along with General Oglethorpe, and John courted a young woman who rejected his attentions. Disillusioned, the two brothers returned to England.[15]

Back in London, John and Charles encountered another Moravian preacher, Peter Boehler. Boehler preached that a personal conversion experience was necessary for salvation. On May 21, 1738, Charles made his profession of faith, and three days later John recorded his experience in his journal:

> *Wednesday, May 24, 1738. In the evening I went very unwillingly to the Society in Aldersgate Street, where one was reading Luther's preface to the Epistle to the Romans. About a quarter before nine, while he was describing the change wrought by God in the heart through faith in Christ, I felt my heart strangely warmed. I felt I did trust Christ, Christ alone, for salvation.[16]*

Soon after his conversion John visited Count von Zinzendorf and the Moravian community at Herrnhut. The Moravians impressed Wesley with their piety and unity.

WESLEY'S METHODS

After visiting Germany, John Wesley preached to many Anglican churches and religious societies, proclaiming the need for a conscious commitment to Christ and the need to grow more like Christ each day. Many pastors objected to his message and refused to allow John to return to their pulpits. They objected to the emotional way the crowds reacted to Wesley's messages.[17]

---

15. Ibid., and Robert C. Walton, *Chronological and Background Charts of Church History* (Grand Rapids: Zondervan Publishing House, 1986), 46.

16. Albert Outler, ed., *John Wesley* (New York: Oxford University Press, 1964), 66.

Wesley began preaching outdoors at Bristol in 1739. Thereafter, he traveled widely throughout England, Ireland, and Scotland. He preached whenever and wherever he could, often from horseback. He traveled five thousand miles a year and preached an average of fifteen sermons each week. Normally, he asked permission to preach from the local Anglican priest. When refused permission, Wesley preached anyway. One priest challenged him saying, "This is not your parish." Wesley replied, "The world is my parish."[18]

Societies. Wesley took his evangelistic technique from George Whitefield but added his own innovations. Wesley established groups that met weekly. These developed into the Methodist societies that Wesley modeled after the cottage prayer meetings of the Pietists. The society in each area was divided into classes, and the members of the classes were instructed to encourage and look after each other. Lay people led the groups, and Wesley appointed preachers to visit the societies on their regular "circuit." Wesley did not see these societies or classes as churches. Instead, he insisted that they represented a valid renewal movement within the Church of England. He expected them to supplement the local church, not to replace it.[19]

Chapels. Wesley's second innovation was meeting houses, or as he called them, chapels. These were simply meeting places for the Methodist society in each area. As the movement grew, the homes of members could not accommodate the members, so Wesley encouraged the construction of the chapels. He did not consider these to be churches, but rather renewal centers that would aid the work of the local church.[20]

John Wesley did not set out to establish a new denomination. Leaving the Church of England never entered his mind in the beginning. He organized his "societies" to provide discipleship training for Christians. Each society was composed of classes of twelve members. New members attended on probation, and all

17. Kenneth Scott Latourette, *A History of Christianity* (New York: Harper & Row, 1953), 1025-27.
18. Ibid.
19. Rudnick, *Speaking the Gospel,* 140.
20. Ibid.

members gave one penny each week. Wesley appointed stewards to care for the chapels and the money. By 1744 the societies had multiplied to the point that Wesley decided to hold annual conferences for the leaders. In 1746 he divided the societies into circuits and appointed preachers to make the rounds of the circuits. A superintendent directed the affairs of each circuit.[21]

Lay preaching. John Wesley was disturbed when some of his Methodist laymen began to preach, and he asked them to stop. However, his mother intervened on their behalf. Susanah told John that by preventing them from preaching he might be opposing the work of the Holy Spirit. Wisely, he listened to his mother, and lay preachers became a distinctive characteristic of Methodism. Eventually, Wesley organized his preachers into conferences which met annually. As his movement grew, he appointed regular preachers to ride the circuits mentioned above. As always, Wesley maintained tight personal control of all the parts of the organization.[22]

Methodist organization. The Methodist movement did not break sharply from the Church of England; instead, as the societies increased in number and acquired property, the movement gradually drifted away from Anglicanism. By 1759 many people spoke of the movement as the Methodist Church, much to Wesley's dismay. After the American Revolution Methodists in the United States were embarrassed by their association with the Church of England. Therefore, Wesley ordained Thomas Coke as the first Methodist bishop in the United States and authorized the organization of the Methodist denomination in America. In 1795, four years after John's Wesley's death, the Methodist church officially withdrew from the Church of England.[23]

WESLEY'S DOCTRINE

Wesley's preaching and doctrine were simple and direct. He invited people to join Methodist societies if they wanted "to flee from the wrath to come, to be saved from their sins." Wesley expected his Methodists to abstain from cursing, unseemly speech, stealing, and

---

21. Starkes, *God's Commissioned People*, 148.
22. Latourette, *History of Christianity*, 1027.
23. Starkes, *God's Commissioned People*, 148.

drunkenness. He urged them to live frugally so that they could give to the church and to charity. He encouraged them to attend the society's meetings where they could hear God's Word.[24]

Writers often summarize Methodist theology as universal salvation, free salvation, sure salvation, and full salvation. These four points correspond to justification by grace alone, true freedom of the human will, assurance through the witness of the Holy Spirit, and sanctification. Wesley taught that a Christian can grow in grace to the place where he reaches perfection. By this Wesley meant that a believer can reach the point that he does not sin voluntarily. Wesley wrote the Twenty-Five Articles to summarize Methodist doctrine and to serve as a guide for the societies.[25]

Undoubtedly, John Wesley was one of the great evangelists of all time. In 1790, the year before his death, Methodists reported 71,668 members in England alone. In his ministry of itinerant evangelism Wesley traveled more than 250,000 miles, mainly by horseback, to spread the gospel. He also preached 40,000 sermons and produced 200 written works.

Five things characterized his successful ministry: (1) zeal in preaching, especially to the middle and lower classes; (2) a tightly knit organization; (3) an emphasis on education; (4) social service; and (5) the use of laity in ministry. John Wesley renewed the church's emphasis on the new birth, the disciplined Christian life, warmhearted preaching, close fellowship, and hymn singing. Certainly, Wesley's ministry lives on wherever there is Bible reading, social concern, missions consciousness, and a love for hymn singing.[26]

CHARLES WESLEY AND REVIVAL MUSIC

James Townsend wrote an article about Charles Wesley entitled, "The Forgotten Wesley;" and, unfortunately, that is often true. Today Charles Wesley is remembered only for his hymns,

---

24. Ibid.

25. Carl S. Meyer, *The Church: From Pentecost to the Present* (Chicago: Moody Press, 1969), 229.

26. Latourette, *History of Christianity*, 1027.

but he was a key figure in the great revival that swept the British Isles.[27]

Charles was born in 1708, five years after John. Like John he grew up in Epworth and went to Oxford University. While a student at Oxford, Charles founded the Holy Club. This club encouraged its members to awake early in the morning for Bible study and prayer and to engage in prison ministry. Charles was an able student at Oxford, eventually earning the master of arts degree. After graduation he went with John to Georgia to serve as chaplain and secretary to Governor Oglethorpe. He spent a miserable year in Georgia and gladly returned to England saying, "I went to America to convert the Indians, but, oh, who will convert me?"[28]

When he returned to England, Charles agreed to teach English to Peter Boehler, the Moravian evangelist. While Charles taught Boehler English, Boehler taught Charles the way to salvation. On May 17, 1738, Charles read Martin Luther's commentary on Galatians. He wrote in his journal, "I laboured, waited, and prayed to feel 'who loved me, and gave himself for me' (Gal. 2:20)." Four days later, while sick in bed, Charles Wesley heard a member of the household say, "In the name of Jesus of Nazareth, arise, and believe, and thou shalt be healed of all infirmities." That verse struck a responsive chord, and he wrote in his journal, "I now found myself at peace with God, and rejoice in hope of loving Christ." Two days later he began writing a hymn about conversion; and when John happily announced his own conversion, the two brothers sang the new hymn together.[29]

Historians often speak of Whitefield as the preacher of the revival, John Wesley as the organizer, and Charles Wesley as the hymn writer. That is not a distortion of the facts, but Charles was also a fine preacher and evangelist in his own right. In his journal Charles estimated that he preached to 149,400 people between 1739 and 1743. In July of 1738 he preached to ten thousand at Moorfields, and twenty thousand at Kennington Common. When

27. James Townsend, "The Forgotten Wesley," *Christian History* 10, No. 3, 6.

28. Ibid., 7.

29. Ibid.

invited to preach at Oxford, he delivered a sermon on justification by faith. He carried on his own itinerant preaching tours until 1756, when ill health forced him into the more settled life of a pastor.[30]

Though gifted as a preacher, Charles's greatest gift was hymn writing. He wrote an average of ten lines of poetry each day and composed a total of 8,989 hymns, ten times as many as Isaac Watts. He published fifty-six volumes of hymns in fifty-three years. These hymnals included hymns that are still favorites today:

"Hark the Herald Angels Sing"

"And Can It Be,"

"O for a Thousand
Tongues to Sing"

"Love Divine, All Loves Excelling"

"Jesus, Lover of My Soul"

"Christ the Lord Is Risen Today"

"Rejoice! The Lord Is King!"

Charles and John Wesley taught their converts to sing, and Methodists became known for their enthusiastic hymn singing. Some scholars have held that the Methodists learned as much doctrine from Charles' hymns as they did from John's sermons and books. Charles Wesley richly deserves the title of the "greatest hymn writer of all ages." He put the revival to music and preserved it for the ages.[31]

THE REVIVAL BEYOND METHODISM

The revival in the British Isles was not limited to the followers of John Wesley. George Whitefield split with John Wesley over theological issues. Wesley was an Arminian in his theology, while

---

30. Ibid.
31. Ibid., 6-8.

Whitefield was a Calvinist. Whitefield and his patroness, the Countess of Huntingdon, founded the Calvinistic Methodist church. The revival also spread to Congregational and Baptist churches. The influence of the revival led William Carey and other British Baptists to establish the Baptist Missionary Society.

The revival also affected the Church of England. An evangelical faction developed within the Anglican Church that has continued until today. Prominent leaders of the faction included John Newton, composer of "Amazing Grace," and Henry Venn, the famous mission administrator. In later years members of the evangelical faction such as William Wilberforce exercised great influence in religious and social reform.[32]

INTERPRETATION AND APPLICATION

Many historians believe that the revival so changed life in England that a violent revolution such as that in France was avoided. The revival certainly improved public morality and prepared the way for the reform movement that helped improve social and economic conditions in Great Britain.[33]

The British revival was an extension and development of Pietism. The common emphases between the two movements are obvious: practical holiness, personal Bible study, need for conscious conversion, evangelistic preaching, devotional exercises, relief of the poor, and the elevation of experience over doctrine. Yet the Wesleys took Pietism to new heights. They popularized Pietism and organized it for permanence and greater effectiveness.

The eighteenth-century revival has lessons for Christians today.

1. *The lives of John and Charles Wesley show the necessity of born-again ministers.* Before their conversions they failed miserably; but after they were saved, they succeeded remarkably.

---

32. Latourette, *History of Christianity*, 1029.

33. Robert Baker, *A Summary of Church History* (Nashville: Broadman Press, 1959, rev. ed. 1994), 299.

2. *George Whitefield and the Wesleys were willing to try a new technique, open-air preaching.* Evangelists today should experiment to discover new ways to communicate Christ effectively.

3. *The personal morality of Whitefield and the Wesleys set an example for itinerant evangelists today.* Not only did they preach the gospel to thousands, but they allowed no hint of moral or financial scandal in their dealings.

4. *John Wesley demonstrated the value of organization.* Though many view organization as unspiritual, he understood that organization helps to channel religious fervor and conserve evangelistic results. Wesley used his Methodist societies to provide follow-up and discipleship training for new converts. Mass evangelists of this century have learned that evangelistic campaigns have little lasting impact unless they incorporate some type of follow-up into their plans. This means there must be some organization to ensure that the necessary things are accomplished.

5. *Charles and John Wesley used music effectively to reach and teach their converts.* They understood that music was a powerful medium that could be utilized in evangelism. Evangelists today do well to remember that the sermon is not the only part of an evangelistic sermon. In fact, the audience may continue to sing hymns or praise songs long after they have forgotten the preacher's message. Truly, Christian worship would be much poorer today had it not been for the Wesleys, and the same can be said for evangelism. The Wesleys and George Whitefield brought the gospel to the masses.

STUDY QUESTIONS

1. What three movements prepared the way for the British revival?

2. What innovations did George Whitefield introduce to evangelism?

3. How did the Pietists influence John Wesley?

4. What two innovations did John Wesley introduce?

5. How would you summarize John Wesley's theology?

6. What contribution did Charles Wesley make to the revival?

7. How did Wesley's movement affect other denominations?

⊷9⊷

The Great Awakening

A remarkable revival movement swept through the British colonies of North America between 1720 and 1744. Historians call it the Great Awakening. The revival transformed the religious and moral character of North America and shaped the nature of American Christianity. To this day American evangelism bears the imprint of the Great Awakening.

From a broad historical perspective the Great Awakening was part of a general awakening that affected Great Britain and northern Europe. As William Warren Sweet explained:

> What we have come to call pietism lies at the heart of great colonial awakenings. By pietism, we mean a type of religion which places the principal emphasis upon what is often termed a religion of the heart, rather than a religion of the head. It is a religion which appeals primarily to the emotions. Its principal theme is redemption for individuals. Its object is to awaken men and women to a personal repentance.[1]

The general awakening had three phases between about 1675 and 1750. The first phase was the development of Pietism

---

1. William Warren Sweet, *Revivalism in America* (Nashville: Abingdon Press, 1944), 24-25.

113

in Germany and Holland. The second phase was the revival in the American colonies, and the third phase was the revival in Great Britain discussed in the previous chapter.

THE NEED FOR REVIVAL

Though several of the American colonies, particularly in New England, had been settled by devout Christians seeking religious liberty, the piety of the people gradually declined until 1700, when daily life was dominated more by taverns than by churches. Even in New England, many people did not concern themselves with church membership or church activities. In 1702 Increase Mather lamented: "Oh New England, New England! tremble, for the glory is going: it is gradually departing."[2]

Part of the problem in New England stemmed from the "half-way covenant." The Puritan churches of New England had forged a middle way between the practices of the Presbyterians and the Baptists. The Presbyterians believed in infant baptism, while Baptists insisted on baptism only for mature believers. The Puritans did baptize the children of members, but they limited applicants for full communicant membership to those who could give testimony of personal salvation. This debate raged on for many years, and some churches were more Presbyterian and some more Baptist. Finally, in 1662, a church synod declared the Half-Way Covenant which allowed any baptized parent to bring a child for baptism in the church. In this way many unsaved people became members of the church. Naturally, this led to a gradual decline in piety on the part of the general population of New England.[3]

The situation was even worse in the middle and southern colonies. Most of these colonies began as commercial ventures, and their settlers had never pretended to be devout. With no bishop to supervise them, many Anglican clergymen neglected their duties, and many of their parishioners forgot to pay their pastors. In most parts of the American colonies religion was a

---

2. Nathan Hatch, Mark Noll, and John Woodbridge, *The Gospel in America* (Grand Rapids: Zondervan Publishing House, 1979), 139.

3. Sidney Ahlstrom, *A Religious History of the American People* (New Haven: Yale University Press, 1972), 158-60.

concern of the few, not the masses. Drunkenness, immorality, and disregard of God and His commandments were all too common. Thomas Bacon, a pastor in the colonies, observed, "Religion among us seems to wear the face of the country, partly moderately cultivated, the greater part wild and savage."[4]

THE FIRST STIRRINGS OF REVIVAL

Many scholars believe the Great Awakening began with the arrival of Theodore J. Frelinghuysen (1691-1747) in America. George Whitefield said of Frelinghuysen: "He is a worthy soldier of Jesus Christ and was the beginner of the great work which I trust the Lord is carrying on in these parts."[5]

FRELINGHUYSEN

Theodore J. Frelinghuysen was born in Germany and educated in Holland. He absorbed pietistic teachings during his theological training and was ordained as a pastor in the Dutch Reformed Church. In 1719 church officials sent him to New Jersey to pastor four Dutch Reformed churches in the Raritan valley. Upon his arrival Frelinghuysen was shocked to discover that most of his members were very casual about their Christian commitment, and many could not give testimony of personal conversion. The young pastor set out to rectify these problems through strong evangelistic preaching, personal witnessing in the members' homes, and withholding communion from those whose lives were undisciplined. He wanted to see his members converted and to help them understand that church membership was more than a cultural norm. He proclaimed from his pulpit that outward religiosity was no substitute for personal conversion. He went further when he declared that church membership would not save a person from hell.[6]

---

4. Hatch, *The Gospel in America*, 139, and Sweet, *Revivalism*, 23-24.

5. Hatch, *The Gospel in America*, 28, and Winthrop Hudson, *Religion in America* (New York: Charles Scribner's Sons, 1965), 62.

6. Hudson, *Religion in America*, 62-63.

Frelinghuysen's activities caused a stir among his church members, who were accustomed to sleeping through boring lectures on Calvinistic theology each Sunday, and who believed that correct doctrine and correct church membership guaranteed salvation. Frelinghuysen's emphasis on conversion and Christian living came as an unwelcome surprise to many members, who opposed his candid preaching and his personal confrontations. Dutch Reformed pastors in New York opposed his ministry and encouraged his members to do the same. However, as more and more of his members made personal commitments to Jesus Christ, opposition began to decline. By 1726 the revival was at its height and began to spread to other Dutch Reformed churches and to other denominations as well.[7]

TENNENT

Gilbert Tennent (1703-64), a Presbyterian minister, became pastor of the Presbyterian church in New Brunswick, New Jersey in 1726. He became acquainted with Frelinghuysen and quickly realized they shared the same desire for revival. At Frelinghuysen's encouragement Tennent began to boldly preach repentance to his members. He believed "presumptuous security" to be his people's main problem. By this he meant that they had been baptized, catechized, and accepted as full members of the church, but they did not understand the meaning of salvation. They knew salvation came through faith, but they interpreted faith as agreement with correct doctrine. They knew the doctrine of Christianity, but they did not know Christ personally. To solve this problem, Tennent began preaching for "conviction." He challenged his hearers to repent and believe the gospel or suffer the torments of hell. He declared that everyone had to experience the terror of lostness in order to know the joy of salvation through Christ's forgiveness. Under Gilbert Tennent's leadership the revival swept through the Presbyterian churches of New Jersey and New York.[8]

---

7. Ibid., 64.
8. Ibid., 64.

The work of revival was also taken up by Gilbert's father and brothers. William Tennent, Gilbert's father, was almost elected president of Yale University. Perhaps in disappointment, he founded his "log college" at Neshaminy, Pennsylvania. There he trained a generation of Presbyterian pastors in sound theology and concern for the lost. Gilbert's brothers, John and William, Jr., also participated in the revival, but Gilbert had the greatest influence both through his public preaching and his printed sermons, which were widely distributed throughout the colonies.[9]

REVIVAL IN NEW ENGLAND

Historians associate the revival in New England with the ministry of Jonathan Edwards. Edwards, a brilliant scholar, graduated from Yale at age seventeen. After serving for several years as a tutor at Yale, Edwards went to Northampton, Massachusetts in 1727 to assist his grandfather, Solomon Stoddard, at the church there. When his grandfather died two years later, Edwards became the senior pastor. Edwards expressed serious concern about the low level of morality shown by his members, especially the youth. He recorded:

Many of them [were] very much addicted to night walking, frequenting the tavern, and lewd practices. It was their manner very frequently to get together in conventions of both sexes for mirth and jollity, which they called frolics, and they would often spend the greater part of the night in them.[10]

To deal with these problems, Edwards began to visit the young people in their homes. Gradually, he saw improvement in their behavior and an increased concern about spiritual things. The breakthrough to revival came through Edwards's preaching. This is rather surprising since he was not what one thinks of as a revival preacher. His sermons emphasized closely reasoned doc-

---

9. Ibid., 64.
10. Ibid., 64.

trine, and they lasted as long as two hours. Edwards read his sermons from manuscript and used few gestures. Still, it was during a series of sermons on justification by faith that fire fell upon Northampton. Apparently, Edwards was as surprised as his people, but there was no denying the movement of the Holy Spirit. During the revival three hundred people were added to his church.[11]

Edwards recorded the events of the revival in his book, *A Faithful Narrative of the Surprising Work of God*. Edwards described the reaction of the people of Northampton:

> *There was scarcely a single person in the town, old or young, left unconcerned about the great things of the eternal world. . . . [S]ouls did, as it were, come by flocks to Jesus Christ. . . . [T]he town seemed to be full of the presence of God: it was never so full of love, nor of joy, and yet so full of distress, as it was then. There were remarkable tokens of God's presence in almost every house.*[12]

News of the revival spread throughout the area. Soon the surrounding towns in Connecticut and Massachusetts were swept up in the revival also. Eventually, forty towns experienced revival. In each case the local pastor led the revival. The revival began to wane in 1737, and was over by 1738. Nevertheless, the level of commitment on the part of the church members continued on a higher plane than before. Many Christians on both sides of the Atlantic read Edwards's *Narrative* and longed for a similar experience of the Spirit's power.[13]

An intriguing question still remains—What brought on the revival? John Wesley said of the revival: "Surely this is the Lord's

---

11. Hatch, *The Gospel in America*, 139-40.

12. Tim Dowley, *Eerdmans' Handbook to the History of Christianity* (Grand Rapids: Eerdmans Publishing Co., 1977), 439.

13. Ahlstrom, *Religious History*, 283, and Milton L. Rudnick, *Speaking the Gospel Through the Ages* (St. Louis: Concordia Publishing House, 1984), 129.

doing and it is marvelous in our eye." Jonathan Edwards agreed with Wesley on that point. Edwards said that it was a sovereign work of God, a miracle of grace. People may pray and prepare their hearts, but God determines the time to send down "showers of blessings." Still, Edwards mentioned two preparatory events. First, two people in the nearby town of Pascomuck died suddenly, reminding the townspeople of the fragility of human life. Second, the dramatic conversion of a woman described by Edwards as the "greatest company-keeper in the whole town" electrified the community. To these one could add the pointed preaching of Edwards, that reminded the people of the necessity of personal conversion. As Edwards said, "Our people do not so much need to have their heads stored, as to have their hearts touched."[14]

George Whitefield and National Revival

George Whitefield unified the colonies in the experience of revival, and he also joined the American awakening to the revival in Great Britain. Whitefield was rightly called the "Grand Itinerant," for he preached to large and responsive crowds in all the American colonies and throughout England as well. Whitefield made seven trips to America, preaching from Georgia to Maine. William Warren Sweet wrote, "He probably preached to more people than any other single preacher of the English speaking world during the eighteenth century." Whitefield joined the revivals in the colonies and Great Britain because he alone had a part in all of them.[15]

New England

Whitefield enjoyed his greatest success in 1739 and 1740. Whitefield was already famous in England because of his open-air preaching in Bristol and London. Upon arriving in America, he made a successful tour through the middle colonies. In the fall of 1740 Whitefield traveled to New England for a series of meetings there. The people of New England were eager to hear this young

14. Hatch, *The Gospel in America*, 139-40, and Sweet, *Revivalism*, 30.
15. Sweet, *Revivalism*, 32-33.

preacher because they had read many newspaper articles about his meetings as well as his published sermons. By any standard Whitefield's tour of New England was remarkable. In 73 days he traveled 800 miles and preached 130 sermons.[16]

Whitefield attracted large crowds everywhere he went. He often preached in the open air because no hall could accommodate the crowd. Many came out of curiosity because of Whitefield's famous voice. He could project his voice so thousands could hear, and he could also inject great pathos into his tone. In fact, someone joked that Whitefield could move a crowd to tears by simply saying "Mesopotamia." Whitefield attracted people from all walks of life, including a skeptical Benjamin Franklin who heard him in Philadelphia. Whitefield's style of preaching differed from most preachers of that day in that he preached extemporaneously. That is, he did not preach from a prepared manuscript. His interesting sermons and appeal to all denominations combined to make him the most popular preacher of colonial America.[17]

The revival produced many tangible results. The earlier revival led by Jonathan Edwards had been confined to the Connecticut River valley, but this later revival affected all of New England. As showers of blessings fell, "nearly everyone got wet," as Edwin Gaustad observed. The people of New England exchanged the religion of routine for a true commitment to Christ. The revival in Boston continued for eighteen months, and during that time thirty religious societies were organized. Perhaps as many as fifty thousand new members were added to the churches, now filled every Sunday. When Whitefield left Boston, he preached to twenty thousand people at his farewell service. He called his friend Gilbert Tennent to continue the revival preaching in his absence.[18]

THE SOUTH

The Great Awakening touched the southern colonies as well. Whitefield preached throughout the South as he had done in New

---

16. Hatch, *The Gospel in America*, 140.

17. Rudnick, *Speaking the Gospel*, 129.

18. Ibid.; Dowley, *Eerdmans' Handbook*, 439-41; and Hatch, *The Gospel in America*, 140.

England. The Awakening radically changed Southern religious life. The Anglican Church (Church of England) had been the established and dominant church in the region since the colonies were founded. However, the Great Awakening brought to those colonies the Baptist and Methodist churches that emphasized aggressive evangelism and individualism. These churches appealed to the lower and middle classes, who thought of themselves as Americans. Their organization and polity suited them for growth on the frontier.[19]

A good example of the appeal and dynamism of the new Baptist churches in the South is the church at Sandy Creek, North Carolina. Sandy Creek was located strategically at the intersection of three major roads. Shubal Stearns, Daniel Marshall, and a congregation of Baptists settled at Sandy Creek in 1755. The little church soon had a big impact on the backcountry of North Carolina. Stearns and Marshall preached in almost every part of the colony and recorded many conversions wherever they went. They refused to accept pay for their ministry, and this helped them win the confidence of the settlers. Morgan Edwards described the results of God's work through the church in this way:

> *Sandy Creek church is the mother of all the Separate Baptists. From this Zion went forth the word, and great was the company of them who published it: it, in 17 years, has spread branches westward as far as the great river Mississippi; southward as far as Georgia; eastward to the sea and Chesapeake Bay; and northward to the waters of the Potomac; it, in 17 years, is become the mother, grandmother, and great-grandmother to 42 churches, from which sprang 125 ministers.[20]*

19. Sweet, *Revivalism*, 35.
20. Quoted in Robert Baker, *A Baptist Source Book* (Nashville: Broadman Press, 1966), 20.

The accomplishments of the Sandy Creek church are all the more remarkable when one remembers how sparsely settled the area was.

OPPOSITION TO THE REVIVAL

Every religious movement has its proponents and opponents, and the Great Awakening was no exception. Many established pastors felt threatened when outside preachers came into their areas. Others simply reacted to a change in the status quo. However, some radical revivalists caused controversy by publicly attacking area pastors. One example of this was James Davenport, an itinerant revivalist of unstable mind. His wild, critical preaching provoked many pastors to oppose the revival in general. These opponents, called "Old Lights," were mainly pastors of Congregational churches in New England. They criticized the revivalists (New Lights) for their enthusiasm, emotionalism, irresponsible itinerancy and criticism of other ministers. Charles Chauncy of Boston was the leader of the Old Lights.[21]

Both Old Lights and New Lights used extreme language and actions in the controversy. Gilbert Tennent's sermon, *The Danger of an Unconverted Ministry*, particularly aroused the anger of the Old Lights. Whitefield described some of the opposition pastors as "dead men speaking to dead congregations." Not surprisingly, many Old Light pastors refused to allow revivalists to preach from their pulpits. The controversy increased to the point in 1744 that it stifled the Awakening in New England, even though the New Lights were more numerous. Nevertheless, the revival continued for some years in the South.[22]

THE RESULTS OF THE GREAT AWAKENING

The Great Awakening produced many and varied results:

1. *Democracy.* The revival promoted the development of democracy through its emphasis on individual deci-

---

21. Rudnick, *Speaking the Gospel*, 129.
22. Hatch, *The Gospel in America*, 141.

sions and the attendant development of churches that featured congregational church government.

2. *Unification of the colonies.* The Great Awakening served to unify the colonies and increase their awareness of each other. In this the revival prepared the way for the American revolution.

3. *Individualistic religion.* The Awakening set the tone for American religious history. The revival emphasized the need for personal conversion. This set well with a nation of rugged individualists.

4. *Upsurge in Baptist and Methodist churches.* The Baptists and Methodists endorsed the revival, and they gained the most from it. Many of the New Lights left Old Light churches to organize separatist churches where revival preachers were welcome. Many of these separatist churches became Baptist. For example, during the Great Awakening the number of Baptist churches in Massachusetts increased from six to thirty; in Connecticut, from four to twelve; and in Rhode Island, from eleven to thirty-six. These two denominations gained members because their informal worship style and aggressive approach to evangelism dovetailed with the thrust of the revival.[23]

5. *Many converts.* It is hard to estimate the number of people who were saved during the Awakening. If records were kept, most of them have been lost. However, Sweet estimated that as many as forty thousand new members were added to New England's churches during the awakening.[24]

6. *Many new churches.* Between 1740 and 1760 one hundred and fifty new Congregational churches were

23. William Warren Sweet, *The Story of Religion in America.* (New York: Harper & Brothers, 1950),
24. Sweet, *Revivalism,* 31.

organized in New England. Many Separatist and Baptist churches were organized as well.[25]

7. *New schools.* As a result of the Awakening several educational institutions were founded, especially for the training of ministers. These included Princeton College and Dartmouth College.

8. *Improved morality.* Throughout the colonies the awakening raised the level of public morality.

9. *Revival meetings.* Because of the Great Awakening the revival meeting became the most common method of evangelism in North America.[26]

10. *Preaching.* The revival popularized a new type of preaching—extemporaneous preaching. George Whitefield introduced it, and many preachers copied his method.[27]

INTERPRETATION AND APPLICATION

In a sense the Great Awakening surged through the colonies in two waves. The first wave was the exciting preaching tours of George Whitefield, Gilbert Tennent, and the erratic James Davenport. Many other itinerants imitated their style. The second wave was the increased evangelistic activity of local pastors. The pastors intensified their efforts at personal evangelism and began to preach more fervently as Whitefield had done. The first wave attracted more notice, but the second wave had a more lasting effect. Regular ministers reaped most of the revival's harvest. This has been true in most revivals in church history. Evangelists like Whitefield played an important part in exciting and focusing public attention on spiritual matters, but people need the personal touch that a local pastor and congregation can give.[28]

---

25. Ibid.
26. Hudson, *Religion in America*, 59.
27. Ibid.
28. Ahlstrom, *Religious History*, 286.

The Great Awakening introduced new methods to American evangelism. These included itinerant preaching, extemporaneous preaching, and extemporaneous prayer. These had been used in previous eras, but their usefulness was rediscovered during the Great Awakening. Whitefield set the example for innumerable traveling evangelists who followed him. American preachers quickly picked up his informal style of preaching which allowed the preacher to hold the audience's attention and sway their emotions.[29]

The revival also set the pattern for American Christianity. Throughout American history religion has been seen as a very personal, individual matter. The revival meeting was accepted as the primary means of communicating the gospel. This is still true in many churches today. It may be that the revival meeting was the best method to use when it was the best show in town, but modern churches would do well to evaluate whether revivals continue to produce results comparable to those of the past.

Finally, the revival brought to America the vision of reaching the world for Christ. As Winthrop Hudson has written:

> *This surging tide of evangelical religion supplied the dynamic which emboldened the Protestant churches of America to undertake the enormous task of Christianizing a continent . . . and led both the British and American churches to join forces in a vast mission to the entire non-Christian world.*[30]

STUDY QUESTIONS

1. What was the key issue in the revival in New Jersey?

2. What was Jonathan Edwards's view on the source of revival?

---

29. Earle Cairns, *An Endless Line of Splendor* (Wheaton, Ill.: Tyndale House, 1986), 333.

30. Hudson, *Religion in America*, 60.

3. What role did George Whitefield play in the Great Awakening?

4. Why did Baptists and Methodists benefit more from the revival than did other denominations?

5. Why did the Old Lights oppose the revival?

6. What lasting effects did the revival have on religion in America?

⇌ 10 ⇌

EVANGELISM ON THE AMERICAN FRONTIER

After the Revolutionary War the churches of America faced a daunting challenge. They had to plan and evangelize a whole continent. As the frontier moved westward, so did the churches. One of the first signs of civilization in the West was the log church, erected by a frontier preacher and his tiny congregation. The fascinating story of the church's westward expansion is the subject of this chapter.

METHODIST CIRCUIT RIDERS

The Methodists were particularly successful evangelists on the frontier. The key person in the development of American Methodism was Francis Asbury (1745-1816). John Wesley ordained Asbury as the first bishop of the Methodist Episcopal Church in America. He remained a bachelor in order to give more time to his successful ministry. He traveled continuously, touring Methodist circuits from Georgia to Maine as well as Ohio and Kentucky. During his tenure he ordained three thousand circuit riders. By the time of his death the Methodists numbered about 250,000.[1]

The Methodists succeeded in reaching frontier people for Christ because their doctrine and organization fit the frontier sit-

---

1. M. Thomas Starkes, *God's Commissioned People* (Nashville: Broadman Press, 1984), 149.

uation. The preaching of the circuit riders appealed to the settlers. Methodists preached free grace and free will in contrast to
the limited grace and predestination taught by the Presbyterians.
The frontier Methodists exhorted their hearers to choose Christ,
emphasizing each person's right to be master of one's own fate.
This emphasis on free will complemented the new democracy of
the West which exalted equality.[2]

The Methodists' organization proved ideal in the frontier
setting. All early Methodist preachers carried on an itinerant
preaching ministry. They preached at more than one church,
traveling along regular circuits, preaching in the Methodist societies and classes. The circuits varied in size according to the
number of classes in the area. If there were no existing classes,
the circuit rider attempted to establish them. Normally, there
were twenty to thirty classes in a circuit.[3]

Horace Bishop's experiences along his circuit were typical of
most circuit riders':

> *I preached twenty-eight times a month. I never took
> breakfast and dinner at the same place except on
> Friday, which was laundry day in the country....
> My wardrobe was one end of my saddlebags; my
> bookcase the other end. . . . My 'study' was the
> shade of any tree on the way to my appointments,
> where there was grass for my horse. . . . I slept
> wherever it was convenient, on a sheepskin or my
> Mexican blanket, occasionally on a dirt or a pun-
> cheon floor.[4]*

Circuit riders encouraged and appointed lay preachers to
carry on the local ministry while they were busy along the circuit.
These lay preachers played a great part spreading Methodism on

---

2. William Warren Sweet, *The Story of Religion in America* (New
York: Harper & Brothers, 1950), 219.

3. Ibid.

4. Ross Phares, *Bible in Pocket, Gun in Hand* (Lincoln: University of
Nebraska Press, 1964), 156.

the frontier. Normally, a young man who gave evidence of faith and speaking ability was encouraged to preach some trial sermons. If these efforts pleased the people, then the circuit rider gave the young man an "exhorter's license." Some of the exhorters became circuit riders, but many remained exhorters their whole lives. Most of these lay preachers had little education, but they made up for that in zeal. Two lay preachers, Francis Clark and John Durham, founded the first Methodist classes in Kentucky.[5]

All the Methodist preachers tried to follow the instructions on preaching found in the Methodist Book of Discipline: "What is the best method of preaching? 1) To convince: 2) To offer Christ: 3) To invite: 4) To build up: And to do this in some measure in every sermon." The rapid increase of Methodists on the frontier testifies to how well the preachers followed their instructions.[6]

The frontier people generally did not believe in a paid ministry. Most thought a preacher should be poor and humble. Apparently, Bishop Asbury encouraged this thinking; on one occasion he "prayed to the Lord to keep the preachers poor." Surely that prayer was not needed. Clearly, the circuit riders did not enter the ministry for the money. Before 1800 a circuit rider's annual salary was $64. In 1816 it was raised to $100; however, that was the amount allowed, not necessarily the amount paid. Peter Cartwright reported that an unmarried circuit rider ordinarily received about $40 a year, and married preachers were soon "starved into location."[7]

BAPTIST FARMER-PREACHERS

The frontier Baptists did not possess the organization of the Methodists. However, their simple message, emotional preaching, and flexible polity also suited the frontier setting. In the years following the American Revolution the Baptists grew rapidly. This advance was led by bi-vocational pastors who farmed to support

---

5. Sweet, *Religion in America*, 219.

6. John B. Boles, *The Great Revival* (Lexington: The University of Kentucky Press, 1972), 112.

7. Phares, *Bible in Pocket*, 159.

their families. These farmer-preachers had little formal education, but they did have a conviction of God's call to preach and a holy boldness to proclaim the message of salvation through Jesus Christ.

These early farmer-preachers identified closely with their people, living and working alongside them. Pastors and church members all lived in log cabins with dirt floors. They cleared fields, pulled stumps, and raised barns together. They planted corn and beans and slaughtered hogs after the first hard frost. The pastor understood the needs of his people because they were his needs too.[8]

John Taylor is a good example of a farmer-preacher. Taylor was born into an Anglican family in Virginia. He accepted Christ through the ministry of William Marshall. In 1783 Taylor gathered his wife and children and made a three-month journey by flat boat and horseback to Kentucky. He settled in Woodward County and cleared a farm. He and several other Baptists joined together to establish the Clear Creek Baptist Church. He served the Clear Creek church as pastor for nine years. His farm prospered, and Taylor became a prominent man in the area. He made preaching tours every summer and had a part in founding seven other churches in Kentucky, western Virginia, North Carolina, and Tennessee. All this service was performed without formal training or financial support from churches.[9]

Most new Baptist churches began in the same way the Clear Creek church did. When a farmer-preacher moved into a new community, he would visit the neighbor families to discover whether they were Baptists. He then began holding Sunday meetings at a centrally located cabin or in a clearing. Often the first church building was a log cabin. Most of the early churches took their names from the creeks along which the settlers lived. Thus there are many churches with names like Old Yellow Creek, Turkey Creek, and Stinking Creek throughout Tennessee and Kentucky.[10]

---

8. Ibid., 155.
9. Sweet, *Religion in America*, 216.
10. Ibid., 217.

The preaching of the farmer-preachers pleased the frontier folks. The preachers promised a sweet heaven for those who trusted in Jesus and a hot hell for those who rejected Him. They had no time for ambiguity. A person was either for Jesus or for the devil. This simple message appealed to the people of the frontier, who had little interest in fine doctrinal distinctions. They preferred a simple gospel, boldly proclaimed.

Baptist polity also suited the frontier. Each Baptist church was autonomous, that is, self-governing. This meant the churches could multiply as quickly as they were able. All that was required was the agreement of a group of like-minded believers to form a church. The Baptist pattern of democracy in congregational decisions also appealed to people in the West. Baptists did not need extensive education in order to be ordained. They simply had to demonstrate a divine call to the ministry, a gift for preaching, and a basic knowledge of the Bible in order to receive ordination. These limited requirements meant that the number of farmer-preachers expanded naturally to meet the needs of the growing number of frontier churches. Denominations with stricter requirements for ordination (like the Presbyterians) tended to grow at slower rates.[11]

THE SECOND GREAT AWAKENING

The Second Great Awakening was a revival that swept through the United States from about 1800 until 1830. The revival in the East differed from the revival along the western frontier. This revival was important for several reasons. First, the Awakening helped the new nation avoid the error of deism. Deism is the belief that God created the world, but He is not personally involved with the present world or its inhabitants. This philosophy was very popular in England and France from 1780 to 1800. It gained a great deal of popularity among American intellectuals during this period. The revival also provided the spiritual dynamic that was needed to evangelize the new frontier

11. Robert Baker, *The Southern Baptist Convention and Its People* (Nashville: Broadman Press, 1974), 87.

settlements. The task of taking the gospel to the new towns in the West taxed the resources and imagination of American church-men. They worried about the state of faith and morality on the frontier. The Second Great Awakening ensured that the West would become Christianized and not slip into barbarianism. Finally, the Awakening secured the position of the revival meet-ing as the primary means of evangelizing the lost of North Amer-ica.[12]

Revival in the East

The Second Great Awakening sprang from the Presbyterian church. The first stirrings of revival came at two small back-woods colleges in rural Virginia, Hampden-Sidney and Washing-ton. Like most people in the United States, the students showed little interest in religious life during the difficult days of the revo-lution. However, in 1786 the students at Hampden-Sidney began to demonstrate a great concern about spiritual things. The revival eventually spread to Washington College. These campus revivals produced a generation of Presbyterian ministers who filled lead-ership roles on the frontier and encouraged the camp meetings there. These pastors had both theological training and a great desire to see revival in the churches.[13]

The revival in the Congregational church began at Yale Col-lege. When Timothy Dwight became president of Yale in 1795, he discovered a very distressing situation on the campus. Many stu-dents were professed agnostics who openly ridiculed Christianity. They believed in deism and considered the Bible fiction. President Dwight debated the students in the classroom and in the college chapel. He presented lectures with titles like "The Nature and Danger of Infidel Philosophy" and "Is the Bible the Word of God?" In 1802 he preached a series of chapel sermons on the topic, "Theology Explained and Defended," in which he con-fronted deism. Through his effective use of apologetics, he won

---

12. Winthrop Hudson, *Religion in America* (New York: Charles Scrib-ner's Sons, 1965), 131-33.

13. William Warren Sweet, *Revivalism in America* (Nashville: Abing-don Press, 1944), 119.

the respect of the students. In 1802 a revival broke out on the campus. One third of the student body made professions of faith, and the revival spread to Dartmouth, Williams, and Amherst Colleges. From the colleges the revival spread into the local churches. These campus revivals produced a generation of revivalistic preachers, like Lyman Beecher, for the Congregational church. Adoniram Judson and Luther Rice participated in these campus revivals and later became the first American foreign missionaries.[14]

REVIVAL IN THE WEST

America's population shifted to the West after the Revolutionary War (1776-1783). The turn of the century witnessed a great migration that populated eleven new states within thirty years. One contemporary witness wrote that in one day 236 wagons passed through his village in western Pennsylvania, and they were all headed for Ohio. The migration continued even during the winter as hopeful settlers sought cheap land in the West.[15]

This remarkable population shift caused several problems. The new land had no schools, churches, or public services. The lack of order and restraint led many people to indulge their base desires. One missionary to Ohio told of some people from Connecticut who came from "a land of Bible and sabbaths and ministers and churches, now act like freed prisoners." The same people who faithfully attended church services in New England "deny Christ in this land of sinful liberty."[16]

The biggest problem on the frontier was homemade whiskey. It became a staple drink among the settlers. Everyone drank it—men, women, children, church members, and even preachers. Stores kept open kegs of whiskey by the door, and customers coming in and going out were free to drink a cup. Settlers served it at all the frontier social functions like turkey shoots, barn raisings, and corn huskings. As a result, drunkenness became the

14. Sweet, *Religion in America*, 226.
15. Sweet, *Revivalism*, 112.
16. Ibid., 118.

chief social problem and most common cause of church discipline.[17]

The Second Great Awakening swept into this disturbing scene in 1800. The revival came into Kentucky and Tennessee through the Cumberland Gap. At the invitation of Daniel Boone, Barton Stone and James McGreedy, two Presbyterian preachers, came to the West. Barton Stone began preaching at the Cane Ridge Meetinghouse in Bourbon County, Kentucky. McGreedy preached in Tennessee for two years before settling near Russellville, Kentucky. McGreedy experienced revival at Hampden-Sidney College, and he hoped to bring revival to the frontier.[18]

In June of 1800 McGreedy invited Presbyterians in his area to attend a sacramental meeting at his church, the Red River Meetinghouse. Many Presbyterians lived far from a church and had little opportunity to partake of the Lord's Supper. McGreedy's fiery preaching and the dawn and dusk prayer meetings brought revival. Many people were saved, and many others revived.[19]

The first true "camp meeting" was held the next month at Gasper River. Preachers conducted services in the open air, and the people lived in wagons. This meeting at Gasper River set the pattern that other camp meetings followed. The camps were laid out in circles, rectangles, or horseshoes, depending on the terrain. Settlers built one or more platforms for the preachers and set up plank seats for their listeners. A pen of rails for "seekers" was erected near the platform. Boys called "runners" chased away the stray hogs and dogs. The preachers led services at 11:00 a.m., 3:00 p.m., and 7:00 p.m. These services consisted of hymn singing, preaching, and the invitation time in which the preachers exhorted the people to accept Christ. The preachers led prayer meetings each morning. The people brought their own food and slept in wagons or on the ground. Camp meetings were important

---

17. Ibid.

18. Earle Cairns, *An Endless Line of Splendor* (Wheaton, Ill.: Tyndale House, 1986), 100; and Lewis Drummond, "The Puritan and Pietistic Tradition," *Review and Expositor*, (Fall 1980), 491.

19. Cairns, *Endless Line of Splendor*, 100.

social events for the frontier settlers, many of whom lived in isolated places.[20]

Barton Stone visited McGreedy's meeting at Red River and was impressed. He organized a camp meeting at Cane Ridge near Paris, Kentucky, which lasted from August 6-12, 1801. The estimates of attendance vary widely, but as many as twenty thousand people may have attended. Three dozen Methodist, Presbyterian, and Baptist preachers conducted the services. People came from Kentucky, Tennessee, and Ohio to attend the meeting. The crowd was so large that many different services were conducted at the same time all over the camp ground.

The worship services concluded with exhortation and invitation. The people reacted to these both emotionally and physically. The written accounts tell of people falling, rolling, jerking their heads, barking like a dog, dancing, singing, weeping, and laughing. When interpreting these phenomena, one should remember that these people lived in dangerous circumstances. The camp meeting was a short but intense religious experience. Most of the preachers did not encourage excesses, but they rightly understood that emotions play a valid part in religion. The preachers used the camp meetings as an opportunity to instruct the people in biblical and doctrinal knowledge.[21] The Presbyterians discontinued their use of the camp meeting by 1805, but the Baptists and Methodists continued to hold camp meetings until about 1840. The Methodists called the camp meeting the "Methodist harvest time." Bishop Francis Asbury estimated that four or five hundred camp meetings were held in 1811. Perhaps as many as one thousand were held in 1820. In 1805 Asbury wrote in his journal about successful camp meetings in which many were saved:

> . . . at Duck Creek camp-meeting five hundred souls; at Accomack camp-meeting, four hundred; at Annamessex chapel, in the woods, two hundred; at Sosmerset, Line chapel, one hundred and twenty; at Todd's chapel, Dorset, two hundred; at Carolina

---

20. Ibid., 101.
21. Ibid.

quarterly meeting, seventy-five; all, all these profess to have received converting grace.[22]

In 1808 Asbury recorded the results of a camp meeting held on Deer Creek in Ohio. He wrote, "There were twenty-three traveling and local preachers on the ground," approximately 125 wagons and tents, and about two thousand people.[23]

RESULTS OF THE SECOND GREAT AWAKENING

The camp meetings affected the spread of Christianity on the frontier in several ways:

1. *Thousands were converted.* As mentioned above, the camp meetings were harvest times for evangelists.

2. *Thousands of people joined churches, and general church attendance increased.* Between 1800 and 1802 the six Baptist associations in Kentucky increased their membership from 4,766 to 13,569. From 1800 to 1805 Methodists in Kentucky and Tennessee grew in number from 3,030 members to 10,158. The camp meetings did not begin in South Carolina until 1802, but between 1802 and 1805 Methodists membership increased from 7,443 to 16,089.

3. *Two new denominations came out of the revival.* The Cumberland Presbyterian Church and the Disciples of Christ (Christian Church) both developed as a result of the Awakening.

4. *Baptists and Methodists became the dominant churches in the South.* Though Presbyterians began the camp meetings, they soon abandoned the method. Many Presbyterian ministers distrusted the emotional nature of the camp meeting worship, and they deplored the slight attention given to correct doctrine.

---

22. Ibid.
23. Sweet, *Revivalism*, 130.

Still, Baptists and Methodists continued to use camp meetings to great effect. The use of lay preachers and uneducated preachers enabled the Baptists and Methodists to maintain their church planting momentum along the frontier. By 1850 in the twelve southern states there were 5,298 Baptist churches, 6,061 Methodist churches, 1,647 Presbyterian churches, and only 408 Episcopal churches (315 of these along the Atlantic seaboard).

5. *The revival transformed the moral climate of the frontier.* Public morality improved noticeably after the revival. George Baxter, a Presbyterian leader from Virginia, visited the West in late 1801 and wrote back to a friend:

On my way to Kentucky I was told by settlers on the road, that the character of Kentucky travellers was entirely changed, and that they were now as distinguished for sobriety as they had formerly been for dissoluteness: and indeed, I found Kentucky the most moral place I had ever been in; a profane expression was hardly heard, a religious awe seemed to pervade the country, and some deistical characters had confessed that, from whatever cause the revival might originate, it certainly made the people better. [24]

6. *The revival had a civilizing influence on the frontier.*

7. *The predominant theology of the frontier changed from Calvinism to Arminianism.* The camp meeting preachers emphasized human free will to choose salvation. This Arminian doctrine also affected evangelism. The Awakening featured individualistic evangelism and de-emphasized the value of doctrinal creeds and theological education.

---

24. Boles, *Great Revival*, 186-87.

8. *The revival set the pattern of Christian ethics for the next century.* The revivalistic churches focused on converting individual sinners rather than transforming society. Like the Pietists, the frontier preachers believed that changed people would change society and improve public morality.[25]

INTERPRETATION AND APPLICATION

The Second Great Awakening ensured that the United States would be a Christian nation. It also ensured that the South would be dominated by evangelical churches to the point that it would be called the "Bible Belt." The Awakening transformed the frontier and made it a Christian stronghold.

The camp meetings reinforced the use of the revival meeting as the primary method of evangelism. They also reinforced the individualistic nature of American evangelism. The frontier preachers called upon individuals to publicly profess their personal faith in Christ. This was done in front of all their friends and neighbors, and it made it hard for a person to later "backslide."

The emotional aspects of the camp meetings have received too much attention. Emotional phenomena were common, but they were not the main thing. In fact, fascination with camp meetings in general has caused writers to neglect the dull but essential routine ministry of the frontier churches and pastors. All the evangelical churches on the frontier emphasized conversion and worked hard to bring individuals to that decision. This is a danger for churches today as well. Too many churches rely on revivals as their primary means of evangelism. It seems as if they make an evangelistic effort one or two weeks a year and then neglect evangelism the rest of the time. This surely falls far short of the New Testament pattern.[26]

The camp meetings do, however, remind us of one important factor in evangelism—human emotions. Many modern church

---

25. Ibid., 183-87.
26. Sweet, *Revivalism*, 132.

leaders distrust the emotional element in religion. This seems to deny the importance of emotions in a person's life. Emotions affect everything a person does. The Pentecostal and charismatic churches understand this and provide an outlet for emotions in worship. Granted, everyone does not choose to worship in the same way. Certainly, people come to Christ in different ways. Still, churches do wrong when they ignore the emotional element of religion.

The history of Christianity on the western frontier demonstrates the importance of flexible methods. Baptists and Methodists were flexible enough to adjust to the needs of the frontier people. They adapted their methods to the situation, and they prospered. The message of salvation through Christ never changes, but methods of evangelism must change.

Finally, the frontier experience also illustrates the importance of church planting. Newly settled areas need many new churches. Denominations that planted churches aggressively on the frontier prospered. The same is true today—dynamic denominations continue to plant churches.

STUDY QUESTIONS

1. How did population shifts affect American Christianity after the American Revolution?

2. How did the Second Great Awakening in the West differ from the East?

3. What factors enabled the Methodists and Baptists to prosper on the frontier?

4. How would you describe the nature of religious experience in the camp meetings?

5. How did the camp meetings affect American Christianity?

⇥11⇤

NINETEENTH-CENTURY REVIVALISM

During the 1800s American churches made the revival meeting their standard evangelistic technique. The traveling evangelist also became a fixture of American life. The evangelists of the 1800s brought the rural revivalism of the frontier camp meetings to town. They dressed the revival in new clothes to make it acceptable to city people. The evangelists institutionalized the revival and made it a planned event rather than a surprising outpouring of divine blessing. This chapter focuses on the two most important evangelists of the nineteenth century, Charles G. Finney and Dwight L. Moody.

CHARLES G. FINNEY

FINNEY'S LIFE

Charles G. Finney (1792-1875) was born in New England, but he grew up in Henderson, New York, near Lake Ontario. He decided to become a lawyer and read law in Adams, New York. He attended the local Presbyterian church and apparently led the church choir. In 1821 he began to study the Bible and discuss its teachings with George Gale, the pastor of the local Presbyterian church. One day Finney determined to settle the matter of his salvation. He went into the forest to pray and stayed there all day. In the late afternoon he returned to his room in town and continued to pray. Late in the evening he experienced God's grace and forgiveness as he reported in his own words:

> *The Holy Spirit descended upon me in a manner that seemed to go through me, body and soul. I could feel the impression, like a wave of electricity, going through and through me. Indeed, it seemed to come in waves and waves of liquid love; for I could not express it in any other way.*[1]

Finney began witnessing about his newfound faith immediately. When a client came to the law office, Finney told him to find another lawyer; he intended to become a preacher. With the endorsement of George Gale, the St. Lawrence Presbytery licensed Finney to preach in 1823 and in 1824 assigned him as a missionary in Jefferson County, New York.[2]

Finney's early evangelistic preaching caused little stir. His theology differed from that of most Presbyterians of his day because he did not emphasize predestination. In 1824 he married Lydia Andrews, and it seemed likely they would serve unremarkably in a local church. Everything changed in 1825 when the Finneys visited George Gale at his new pastorate in the town of Western, New York. Gale asked Finney to preach, and the townspeople responded enthusiastically. This success launched Finney's career as a revivalist.[3]

From 1825 to 1831 Finney held revival meetings in the towns of northern and western New York. This area had so many revivals that it was called the "burned over district." Everywhere Finney preached he enjoyed popular support. His tall stature, clear voice, piercing eyes, and passionate delivery endeared him to the people. He drew great crowds, and he challenged them to decide then and there to commit their lives to God. Finney stressed the need for a personal decision for Christ. Finney's

---

1. V. Raymond Edman, *Finney Lives On* (Minneapolis: Bethany Fellowship, 1971), 35-36.
2. James E. Johnson, "Charles Grandison Finney: Father of American Revivalism," *Christian History* 20:6-7.
3. Ibid.

greatest triumph was the meeting he held in Rochester, New York, in 1830-31. Finney's preaching affected the whole city. Shopkeepers closed their stores in order to attend the meetings; the taverns closed for lack of business.[4]

Soon after the Rochester meeting ended, Finney went to New York City as pastor of the Chatham Street Chapel. During his years in the city he delivered a lecture series that was published under the title, *Lectures on Revivals of Religion*. This book became *the* handbook for the next generation of revivalists. In 1835 Finney's wealthy supporters, who included the Tappan brothers, built Broadway Tabernacle for Finney; its circular shape let Finney turn his penetrating gaze on all the people.[5]

In 1835 Finney became a professor at Oberlin College in Ohio. He accepted the position with the intention of splitting his time between the Broadway church and the college. This arrangement did not last long, and Finney devoted more and more of his attention to the college. For many years Finney taught at Oberlin during the fall and spring semesters and then spent the summers conducting revivals in the East. In the 1850s Finney went to England twice to conduct series of revival meetings, and he enjoyed modest success there.[6]

In later years Finney left the Presbyterian church and became pastor of the Congregational church at Oberlin. He devoted most of his time to teaching at the college and preaching at his church. He and Asa Mahan developed a doctrine of Christian perfectionism, and Finney's preaching in his later years mainly focused on that theme. He also became a strong promoter of the abolition movement. These two interests detracted somewhat from his revival preaching, and Finney's later revivals in Boston and Rochester, where he was formerly successful, had disappointing results. Perhaps his preaching on perfectionism confused his audiences. Finney continued to preach and teach at Oberlin College until his death in 1875.[7]

---

4. Ibid. and William G. McLoughlin, *Revivals, Awakenings, and Reform* (Chicago: University of Chicago Press, 1978), 123.

5. Johnson, "Charles Grandison Finney," 8.

6. Ibid.

7. Ibid.

FINNEY'S MESSAGE

Finney reacted strongly against the New England Calvinism of his day. Staunch Calvinists emphasized the sovereignty of God and His election of sinners to salvation. Finney called Calvinism an "old fiction." He developed a personal theology stressing humanity's free will. He believed each person is free to choose or reject Christ. Each individual chooses to go to heaven or to hell. Finney had little patience with excuses for rejecting Christ. He said the sinner's "cannot is his will not. The will is free. . . . [S]in and holiness are voluntary acts of mind."[8]

Finney did not believe in written creeds and confessions. He said creeds must give way to common sense and human experience. He did not speak to people about the effects of Adam's sin upon them; instead, he challenged them to rectify their own sins. He denied total depravity and insisted that people were bound only by their own selfishness and fleshly desires.[9]

Finney summarized the doctrines he preached in his early revivals in his *Memoirs*:

> *The total moral, voluntary depravity of unregenerate man; the necessity of a radical change of heart, through the truth, by the agency of the Holy Ghost; the divinity and humanity of our Lord Jesus Christ; his vicarious atonement, equal to the wants of all mankind; the gift, divinity and agency of the Holy Ghost; repentance, faith, justification by faith, sanctification by faith, persistence in holiness as a condition of salvation. . .*[10]

Finney's preaching was remarkably direct. He preached in a colloquial, personal style. This was a new approach for his day. Sometimes he named individual sinners from the pulpit:

---

8. McLoughlin, *Revival, Awakening, and Reform*, 125.

9. Johnson, "Charles Grandison Finney," 9.

10. William Warren Sweet, *Revivalism in America* (Nashville: Abingdon, 1944), 136.

Oh God, smite that wicked man, that hardened sinner. . . . Oh God, send trouble, anguish and affliction into his bed chamber this night. . . . God Almighty, shake him over hell!

Of course, naming individuals in a small town brought considerable pressure on the sinner to repent. Most sinners did come to the "anxious bench" to get things right with God.[11]

FINNEY'S METHODS

Finney changed both evangelism's methods and the church's concept of revival. Jonathan Edwards and George Whitefield believed that revival is an outpouring of God's blessings in which He awakens Christians. The timing and occasion are in God's hands, and humans can do nothing to affect it. The preacher is merely an instrument used by God. God revives the saints and converts the sinners. In sharp contrast, Finney taught that a revival "is not a miracle, or dependent on a miracle in any sense. It is a purely philosophical result of the right use of the constituted means." Whereas Edwards and Whitefield held a Calvinistic view that emphasized God's work in revival, Finney took an Arminian approach that focused on human actions.[12]

Finney wrought another change in evangelism by bringing mass evangelism to the cities. He introduced the idea of modern mass evangelism and employed it effectively in urban areas. Critics called Finney's progressive methods "New Measures," and these innovations caused a lot of controversy. One of his measures was the "protracted meeting." In Finney's early years evangelistic campaigns lasted for three or four days. Services were conducted every morning, afternoon, and evening. Usually the town shut down during the meetings, which were often held in tents, theaters, auditoriums, or large churches. As the revivals moved into

---

11. McLoughlin, *Revivals, Awakenings, and Reform*, 125.
12. Nathan O. Hatch, Mark Noll, and John Woodbridge, *The Gospel in America* (Grand Rapids: Zondervan Publishing House, 1979), 141; and William G. McLoughlin, *Modern Revivalism* (New York: Ronald Press, 1959), 11.

the cities, the planners had to change the scheduling. Merchants could not afford to close their stores for three or four days when their competitors did not. Therefore, Finney began holding most of his meetings at night and "protracting" them for three or four weeks. Also, most revivalists led services for a particular denomination, but Finney popularized the "union meeting" in which all the churches in town joined together to sponsor the campaign.[13]

Finney employed many other methods that are now commonplace, but they were surprising innovations in his time. He organized groups that met to pray in preparation for his arrival. His lay workers posted handbills and placed advertisements in local newspapers to publicize his campaigns. He trained ministers and active laymen to counsel sinners sitting on the "anxious bench" at the front of the meeting hall. He visited door-to-door to witness to people and invite them to the services. He hired a musician to direct the music at his meetings and encouraged him to use modern music and trained choirs. Mrs. Finney led special services for women, and Finney allowed women to pray aloud in his meetings. Later evangelists refined Finney's methods, but most of them closely followed his example.[14]

FINNEY'S RESULTS

Charles G. Finney was the greatest evangelist of his day. He bridged the period from the Second Great Awakening to the modern era. His campaigns became the model for later evangelists. He is justly called the "father of modern revivalism." Scholars estimate that during his ministry five-hundred thousand people made professions of faith in Jesus Christ.[15]

Finney saw many accept Christ through his evangelistic work. He also felt proud that many of his converts became Christian activists. Finney's converts actively supported the many Christian societies that came into existence during the Second Great Awakening. These included the American Tract Society, the American Bible Society, the American Sunday School Union, and

---

13. McLoughlin, *Revivals, Awakenings, and Reform*, 127.
14. Ibid.
15. Johnson, "Charles Grandison Finney," 9.

others. Finney's converts also took an active part in the temperance movement and the abolition movement. Finney lived long enough to be gratified by these positive and long-term results from his ministry.[16]

Why was Finney such a successful evangelist? The following reasons no doubt contributed:

- Finney had a strong sense of urgency about people's salvation.

- Finney put the Bible first in his thinking and preaching.

- Finney spent hours each day in prayer, usually in the early morning.

- Finney related his sermons to everyday life. He was able to do this because he visited in the community each day.

- Finney was a former attorney who preached for a verdict. He said each person could accept or reject salvation, but he insisted that one does have to decide.[17]

DWIGHT L. MOODY

Dwight L. Moody was the greatest revivalist of the 1800s. He brought new methods and new enthusiasm to evangelism. Moody understood the urban masses and developed evangelistic methods to reach them. Moody built upon Finney's methods and took mass evangelism to new heights of success.

Moody made the "union meeting" synonymous with "revival meeting," especially in the cities. A union meeting emphasized the basic gospel message and played down denominational differences. Normally, the evangelist tried to secure the consent and cooperation of all the evangelical churches of the community. Moody did this very successfully, gaining the enthusiastic support of pastors and wealthy laymen. As a result, he often spoke to

---

16. Sweet, *Revivalism*, 160.
17. Edman, *Finney Lives On*, 11-12.

crowds of ten thousand people. One scholar estimates that Moody presented the gospel to over 100 million persons.[18]

MOODY'S LIFE

Dwight L. Moody (1837-1899) was a creature of the Victorian age, and he did much to preserve the religious and social values that Queen Victoria exemplified. The period spanned by Moody's life saw many social and intellectual developments. However, Moody evoked in many listeners a desire to return to the simpler values and ideas of earlier times.

Nobody in his hometown of Northfield, Massachusetts, would have imagined that Dwight Moody would someday become a world famous evangelist. His father died when Moody was only four, leaving his mother Betsy with the burden of raising nine children on a small farm. His family was poor, and Moody received little education, religious or secular. He received only the equivalent of a fifth-grade education, and he never attended college or seminary. Even after he became a famous preacher, his sermons revealed his limited education. His humble beginnings, though, made Moody a man of the people. He never lost his common touch or basic humility.[19]

Moody despaired at the bleak prospects of the Northfield farm and left for Boston at age seventeen. He secured a job as a clerk in his uncle's shoe store. He joined the local YMCA in order to participate in its social and educational activities. Moody enjoyed the lively social life of Boston and vowed never to return to the farm. He wrote his mother, "I would not go back again to live for nothing."[20]

In order to get his job Moody promised his uncle he would attend church regularly. As good as his word, Moody began attending the Mount Vernon Congregational Church. He joined a Sunday School class for young men, and the teacher, Edward

---

18. McLoughlin, *Modern Revivalism*, 154; David Maas, "The Life and Times of D. L. Moody," *Christian History* 25:5; Kevin Miller, "Delightfully Unconventional," *Christian History* 25:2.

19. Maas, "Life and Times of D. L. Moody," 6.

20. John C. Pollock, *Moody: A Biographical Portrait* (Grand Rapids: Zondervan Publishing House, 1963), 9-11.

Kimball, took a personal interest in young Dwight. On April 21, 1855, Kimball decided to speak to Dwight about his salvation. Kimball went to the shoe store and witnessed to Moody. Kimball described the event this way:

I asked him to come to Christ, who loved him, and who wanted his love and should have it. It seemed that the young man was just ready for the light that broke upon him, for there, at once, in the back of that shoe store in Boston Moody gave himself and his life to Christ.[21]

Soon after his conversion, Moody applied for membership at Mount Vernon Church. The membership committee questioned Moody about his spiritual life and doctrinal beliefs. Moody replied to most of the questions with grunts and monosyllables. Finally, the chairman asked, "Mr. Moody, what has Christ done for us all—for you—which entitles Him to our love?" Moody replied, "I don't know. I think Christ has done a good deal for us. But I don't think of anything particular as I know of." As you might imagine, the committee refused to grant him membership, but they assigned two kindly deacons to instruct him in the faith. The next year Moody applied again and was accepted as a member.[22]

In 1856 Moody decided to move to Chicago to join his cousin Frank. Moody got a job in a shoe store and soon made a mark for himself in the business community. He enjoyed the bustling atmosphere of Chicago and used his savings to invest in land. He joined Plymouth Church and rented four pews, which he filled with store clerks of his acquaintance.[23]

In 1858 Moody personally established a Sunday School at North Market Hall. In 1861 he gave up his business to devote full time to his Sunday School and the YMCA. The Chicago YMCA named Moody as its director, and he proved to be both an effec-

---

21. Ibid., 13.
22. Ibid., 14-15.
23. Ibid., 19.

tive evangelist and an effective fund raiser. He solicited great sums of money from sympathetic businessmen like John Farwell and Cyrus McCormick, who were impressed with Moody's sincerity and drive. After the Civil War began, Moody served effectively as a volunteer chaplain in army camps.[24]

In 1864 Moody founded the Illinois Street Independent Church, known today as Moody Memorial Church. He continued to lead the Chicago YMCA and became a popular speaker at YMCA conventions in America and England. The Great Chicago Fire of 1871 destroyed the church, his home, and the YMCA office. This loss depressed Moody for a time, but he eventually decided he should give himself to preaching rather than committee meetings and fund raising. From 1871 to 1899 Moody devoted most of his time to itinerant evangelism, primarily in large cities.[25]

In 1873 Moody and his song leader, Ira Sankey, conducted evangelistic meetings in England and Scotland. They attracted so much media attention that Moody returned to America as a world famous evangelist. Committees in all the major cities of the United States invited Moody to hold meetings in their cities. From 1875 to 1878 Moody and Sankey led evangelistic campaigns all over the country. Observers estimated the total attendance in New York at 1,500,000 and 1,050,000 in Philadelphia. Of course, many of these were people who attended again and again.[26]

In 1879 Moody redirected his focus from evangelism to education, though he continued to conduct meetings until his death. In 1879 Moody founded Northfield Seminary, an academy for girls, and in 1881 he established the Mount Hermon School for boys. In 1880 he began holding summer Bible conferences at Northfield. The Student Volunteer Movement, a missions movement led by college students, began at Northfield in the summer of 1886. At that meeting one hundred college students committed themselves to serve as foreign missionaries after they graduated. In 1886 Moody founded the Chicago Evangelization Society,

24. Maas, "Life and Times of D. L. Moody," 6.
25. Ibid., 7.
26. Ibid., 8; McLoughlin, *Modern Revivalism*, 265.

which later became the Moody Bible Institute. Moody wanted to enhance the practical training of the students at his Bible institute; therefore, in 1894 he started the Colportage Association. The Association sent out students on horse-drawn "Gospel Wagons" to sell Bibles and religious literature.[27]

In November, 1899 Moody became ill while leading an evangelistic meeting in Kansas City. Friends brought him home to Chicago in a special railway car. Moody's strength ebbed steadily until December 22. On that day Will Moody heard his father say, "Earth recedes, heaven opens before me! No, this is no dream, Will. It is beautiful. It is like a trance. If this is death it is sweet. God is calling me and I must go. Don't call me back!" A few minutes later Moody died. His death fulfilled a prediction he made in New York in August, 1899:

> *Some day you will read in the papers that Moody is dead. Don't you believe a word of it. At that moment I shall be more alive than I am now. . . . I was born of the flesh in 1837, I was born of the Spirit in 1855. "That which is born of the flesh may die. That which is born of the Spirit shall live forever."* [28]

MOODY'S MESSAGE

Dwight Moody preached a simple gospel message, emphasizing a personal relationship with Jesus Christ. He once said, "Christianity is not a dogma; it is not a creed; it is not doctrine; it is not feeling; it is not an impression; but it is a person." Moody saw his responsibility as introducing people to Christ. Untrained in theology, he left doctrinal teaching to others.[29]

On one occasion Moody disclaimed having any theology. A critic once said, "I want to be frank with you, Mr. Moody. I want you to know that I do not believe in your theology." Moody relied,

---

27. McLoughlin, *Modern Revivalism*, 272; Maas, "Life and Times of D. L. Moody," 8.

28. Pollock, *Moody*, 314-317.

29. McLoughlin, *Modern Revivalism*, 250.

"My theology! I didn't know that I had any. I wish you would tell me what my theology is."[30]

Actually, Moody did have a theology. He was essentially a biblicist. He based all his doctrinal beliefs on the Bible. He did not read a lot, though he enjoyed reading the works of Charles Haddon Spurgeon. One could call Moody the "first fundamentalist," and that would be an accurate description. Moody rejected Darwinism and higher criticism of the Bible. He accepted the dispensational premillennialism of J. N. Darby and C. I. Scofield. In fact, Moody was the first prominent evangelist to embrace premillennialism. Most of his predecessors had been postmillennialists. Moody did not develop a detailed eschatology, but he did believe the world was deteriorating and the return of Christ was the only hope for mankind.[31]

Moody's theology can be summarized by three Rs. He believed that mankind was "*Ruined* by the fall." Moody believed strongly in the total depravity of man. Moody said, "I look upon this world as a wrecked vessel; God has given me a lifeboat and said to me, 'Moody, save all you can.'" Moody also believed that mankind was "*Redeemed* by the blood." He preached again and again on the blood atonement of Jesus Christ. He emphasized God's love for sinners which prompted God to provide a substitutionary atonement for those lost in sin. Finally, Moody believed that Christians are "*Regenerated* by the Spirit." Moody did not use high-pressure invitations or manipulate his audiences. He held that the Holy Spirit brought people to conviction, conversion, repentance, and faith. Moody stated, "Every dead soul brought to life must be brought to life by the power of the Spirit. . . . We cannot force inquirers into the kingdom of God. The Holy Spirit must quicken." These three Rs represent Moody's beliefs, but he was more concerned with whom one believes than what one believes.[32]

---

30. Stanley Gundry, "The Three Rs of Moody's Theology," *Christian History* 25:16-19.

31. Ibid; McLoughlin, *Revival, Awakening, and Reform*, 143.

32. Gundry, "The Three Rs of Moody's Theology," 17-19.

MOODY'S METHODS

Dwight Moody made evangelism a big business. That is not to say that evangelism was just a job to him; rather, Moody was the first to apply business principles to evangelism. Moody, the successful businessman, applied the lessons he had learned in the field of commerce to evangelism. Businessmen provided most of the support for his meetings. Moody's innovative techniques made urban, citywide meetings possible. (Finney had preached effectively in New York and Boston.) Even though his greatest success was in small towns, Moody focused on the cities. He said, "Water runs down hill, and the highest hills are the great cities. If we can stir them, we shall stir the whole nation."[33]

Campaign organization. Moody's campaigns were usually conducted along the following lines:

- A committee of pastors and prominent laymen jointly invited Moody to conduct a meeting in their city.

- A steering committee was organized which appointed sub-committees to handle the preparations in regard to finances, prayer, visitation, publicity, music, and others.

- Ushers, choir members, and personal workers (counselors) were trained in advance.

- The committee rented a large auditorium or constructed a temporary "tabernacle."

- Moody and his associates conducted three meetings each day: a morning inspiration service, a noon prayer meeting, and the preaching service in the evening. There were no meetings on Saturday because that was Moody's day to rest.

- Moody never made public appeals for financial support. He left the fund-raising to the committee, and he maintained a simple life-style.[34]

---

33. William Moody, *D. L. Moody* (New York: Macmillan Co., 1930), 194.
34. McLoughlin, *Modern Revivalism,* 231.

Evangelistic innovations. Moody introduced several innovations to revivalism. First, he advertised his campaigns widely. Some criticized Moody for this, but he replied, "Some ministers think it undignified to advertise their services. It is a good deal more undignified to preach to empty pews, I think." Second, Moody introduced the "inquirers' room" to American evangelism. Finney invited those who were anxious about their salvation to sit on the "anxious bench" at the front of the hall. Moody did not use the anxious bench; instead, he invited those who wished to inquire further about salvation to go into the inquirers' room where personal workers waited to counsel with them.[35]

Third, in the later years of his evangelistic ministry Moody's assistants prepared "decision cards." The cards were distributed to the personal workers before the service, and they were instructed to write the inquirers' names, addresses, and church background. This was a significant development because it enabled local pastors to visit the inquirers, and it made it possible to keep accurate records of the meeting's results.[36]

Perhaps Moody's greatest innovation was his use of music in the meetings. Moody used several different musicians in his career, but he worked with Ira Sankey during the 1870s, his most active period of evangelism. Sankey's winsome music attracted many to the meetings. In fact, the humble Moody said, "The people come to hear Sankey sing, and then I catch them in the gospel net." Normally, the crusade committees advertised with this slogan: "Mr. Moody will preach the gospel and Mr. Sankey will sing the gospel."[37]

The meetings usually offered three types of singing. At the beginning of the evening service Sankey would lead the congregation in singing for thirty minutes. Next, the trained choir presented special numbers. Before the sermon, Sankey would sing solos accompanying himself on his pump organ. Sankey wrote a number of gospel songs and popularized others. Perhaps his most popular song was "The Ninety and Nine." Moody's favorite was "Jesus of Nazareth Passeth By." At the conclusion of the sermon Sankey led an invitation hymn to encourage people to go to the inquiry room.[38]

---

35. Ibid., 222.
36. Ibid., 264.
37. Ibid., 233-34.
38. Ibid.

Moody's preaching was notable for its simplicity. He preached simple sermons that any store clerk could understand. His grammar was poor, but Moody made the message clear by using short, simple sentences and lots of illustrations that touched the heart. Moody's sincerity shone through his sermons, and he often wept in the pulpit. Moody was a great storyteller, and many of his messages were simply Bible stories retold and applied to contemporary life. Moody loved a good joke, and he often injected humor into his sermons. Usually, Moody presented topical messages with rather loose outlines. He did not like outbursts and discouraged them in his meetings.[39]

MOODY'S RESULTS

William Warren Sweet described Dwight Moody as the greatest evangelist of the 1800s.[40] Through his evangelistic campaigns, he may have won as many as 100,000 people to Christ. That is a remarkable accomplishment for one who preached before the days of radio and television. Moody conducted his greatest meetings in cities like New York, Chicago, Boston, Philadelphia, San Francisco, Glasgow, and London. The following table gives the estimates of conversions at Moody's early revivals.[41]

City	Duration	Low Estimate	High Estimate
Edinburgh	8 weeks	1,500	7,000
Glasgow	6 weeks	3,200	3,500
London	22 weeks	3,000	7,000
Brooklyn	4 weeks	1,000	2,000
Philadelphia	10 weeks	3,500	12,000
New York	10 weeks	3,500	8,000
Chicago	16 weeks	2,500	10,000

39. Ibid, 239-40.
40. McLoughlin, *Modern Revivalism*, 263.
41. McLoughlin, *Modern Revivalism*, 263.

In his later years Moody held his services in large churches rather than in central tabernacles. This change saved money, but it limited his crowds and decreased the publicity and general enthusiasm.

Moody never generated much enthusiasm among the lower class in England or the United States. He mainly attracted native-born Americans of the middle and upper classes. One Boston newspaper reported that his audience was composed of "the better class of people." Moody did find a following among those who longed for the simple Christianity of times past. Many of his listeners embraced Moody because he rejected evolution and biblical higher criticism.[42]

OTHER PROMINENT EVANGELISTS

A number of evangelists achieved prominence in the late 1800s, though none rivaled Moody's fame.

- *Rodney "Gipsy" Smith* (1860-1947) was a British evangelist who began his ministry with William Booth's Salvation Army. He made several trips to America and gained wide popularity on both sides of the Atlantic.

- *Henry Moorhouse* (1840-1880) was noted not only for his effective preaching but also for his spirituality. He influenced Dwight Moody by teaching him to rely on the Holy Spirit.

- *J. Wilbur Chapman* (1859-1918) was a noted Presbyterian pastor and evangelist. He worked with Moody for a time. He is best known as Billy Sunday's mentor.

- *Sam Jones* (1847-1906), a well-known Methodist evangelist, developed the concept of an evangelistic team. His teams included a soloist, a private secretary, a stenographic reporter to record his sermons, a

---

42. Ibid.

choir leader, an assistant evangelist, and a youth worker. Jones had practiced law in Georgia before he became a Christian, and his humorous illustrations and Southern humor brought him great popularity in the South and Midwest.[43]

Interpretation and Application

Although many traveling evangelists crisscrossed the United States and Great Britain during the 1800s, Finney and Moody dominated the scene. Finney made the revival meeting the primary method of evangelism in America. His *Revival Lectures* became the handbook for American evangelists; it emphasized revival methods rather than the sovereignty of God. Finney insisted that the right methods properly applied would bring results. Jonathan Edwards would have been appalled at Finney's arguments.

Dwight L. Moody brought the revival meeting to the city. He taught evangelicals how to conduct campaigns in urban areas. Moody also demonstrated how to involve lay people in the campaign. His nondenominational approach made it possible to conduct union meetings that enjoyed the support of all the Protestant churches.

Study Questions

1. How was Finney's concept of revival different from that of Jonathan Edwards?

2. What new methods did Finney introduce to revivalism?

3. What did the theology of Finney and Moody have in common?

4. What new methods did Moody introduce to revivalism?

5. Why was Moody so successful?

43. Ibid., 302.

⊰ 12 ⊱

TWENTIETH-CENTURY REVIVALISTS

On April 7, 1917, three thousand people gathered in a train station in New York City to greet Billy Sunday. The next day twenty thousand people crowded into a specially constructed tabernacle on Broadway to hear the famous evangelist. Speaking without the aid of a megaphone or microphone, Sunday said, "I've been preaching for twenty years and I never saw a town with so much vim, ginger, tabasco and peppermint as little old New York." The crowd roared its approval, and the crusade was off and running. What events brought Billy Sunday to this moment of triumph? What forces shaped his life and ministry?[1]

BILLY SUNDAY

SUNDAY'S LIFE

A number of urban evangelists followed Dwight L. Moody: R. A. Torrey, J. Wilbur Chapman, Sam Jones, George Stewart, W. E. Biederwolf, and Billy Sunday. They all imitated Moody in some respects. They all believed in a conservative theology and they all preached a simple gospel anyone could understand. Like Moody, they all used evangelistic singers who sang solos and led great choirs of volunteer musicians. They all set up elaborate

---

1. William L. Coleman, "Billy Sunday: A Style Meant for His Time and Place," *Christianity Today*, 17 December 1976, 14.

organizations to promote and conduct their meetings, and the cost of these meetings went higher and higher. Often, the evangelist demanded that a certain sum be raised before agreeing to come. The greatest of the big-time evangelists in the early twentieth century was Billy Sunday. He perfected the use of business techniques to publicize and organize his campaigns. He claimed to have preached to eighty million people in his career.[2]

Billy Sunday (1862-1935) was born on a farm near Ames, Iowa. His father died, leaving the family destitute. Out of desperation his mother sent Billy to an orphanage when he was ten. He left the orphanage as a teenager and worked at odd jobs. He never acquired much formal education. Billy began playing sandlot baseball and discovered he had a true gift for the game. In 1883 a scout for the Chicago White Stockings signed him to play baseball professionally. He became a star for the Chicago team, making $500 a month, a tremendous sum in those days.

In 1886 Billy Sunday accepted Christ at a street service conducted by the Pacific Garden Mission. He joined the YMCA and became active in Bible study and personal witnessing. His success in evangelism led him to give up baseball for the ministry. After working for a time with the Chicago YMCA, Sunday became J. Wilbur Chapman's assistant and worked in a number of his crusades. In 1896 Sunday began to hold his own meetings in small midwestern towns, preaching on the "kerosene circuit." He preached in churches, tents, warehouses, and wooden tabernacles.[3]

Billy Sunday was not an instant success. He endured several lean years as he perfected his techniques and built his reputation. Gradually, Sunday gained the recognition he desired. His messages on Christ, morality, hard work, the evils of alcohol, and patriotism struck a responsive chord in America. He enjoyed his greatest popularity from 1905 until 1920. Night after night from 15,000 to 20,000 people came to his specially built tabernacles. Many of them accepted his invitation to "hit the sawdust trail"

2. William Warren Sweet, *Revivalism in America* (Nashville: Abingdon Press, 1944), 170-71.

3. William G. McLoughlin, *Revivals, Awakening, and Reform* (Chicago: The University of Chicago Press, 1978), 146.

and be saved. He preached in the chapel at Yale University and dined with Presidents Theodore Roosevelt and Woodrow Wilson. Between 1908 and 1920 Sunday received over one million dollars in "love offerings."[4]

Sunday's popularity reached its peak during World War I. His flag-waving patriotism appealed to a nation at war, but his popularity declined after the war. Criticisms of his luxurious life-style detracted from his message. The secular attractions of the roaring twenties absorbed public attention. As motion theaters and radio developed, the traveling evangelist was no longer the best show in town. Sunday's personal life was free of scandal, but his three sons led troubled lives that embarrassed their father. Furthermore, Sunday failed to adapt his messages to the changing times. He continued to preach crusades until his death in 1935, but he conducted most of his later meetings in small towns in America's heartland.[5]

SUNDAY'S MESSAGE

Billy Sunday preached simple messages. His sermons revolved around the themes of salvation through Christ, old-time religion, the tragic effects of drink, and American patriotism. Sunday had no formal theological education, and he never burdened his audiences with theological lectures. He tried to reduce Christianity to its lowest common denominator so the average person could understand his message.[6]

In regard to Christ, Sunday declared that God had "paid a price" for mankind's salvation by crucifying Christ. Those who refused to accept salvation were refusing to deliver to God what He had purchased. Sunday said, "When you refuse, you are not giving God a square deal." All a person had to do to be saved was to "hit the sawdust trail." This was simply to walk down the saw-dust-covered aisle of a tabernacle or tent, shake Sunday's hand, and fill out a decision card. An assistant then handed the convert

---

4. Grant Wacker, "All American Apostles," *Christianity Today*, 24 June 1991, 36.
5. Ibid.
6. Ibid.

a booklet which stated that by coming forward the person had become a child of God and had received eternal life. Sunday claimed this was the "old-time religion of our fathers."[7]

Billy Sunday often preached on decency, and at times he equated decency with salvation. He stated, "A man will be a Christian if he is decent and if he is not a Christian he forfeits any claim to decency." On another occasion he declared, "Do you believe it's right and manly to be a Christian? Then come on down. If you don't, stay where you are." On still another night Sunday declared, "Come on down and take my hand against booze, for Jesus Christ, for your flag."[8]

Billy Sunday preached his "Booze Sermon" more than any other. He had a deep and abiding hatred for the liquor industry. Sunday told the people of New York, "Whiskey is all right in its place, but its place is in hell. And I want to see everyone put it there as soon as possible." He campaigned actively for prohibition. When prohibition began, he held a mock funeral for "John Barleycorn." Sunday said that alcohol "eats the carpets off the floors, the clothes off of your back, your money out of your bank, food off the table, and shoes off of the baby's feet." At the end of the Booze Sermon Homer Rodeheaver usually led the crowd in singing "De Brewer's Big Hosses Can't Run Over Me."[9]

Billy Sunday identified Christianity with the "American way of life." For Sunday being a Christian and being a good American were synonymous. During World War I he told his audience:

The soldier who breaks every regulation, yet is found on the firing line in the hour of battle, is better than the God-forsaken mutt who won't even enlist, and does all he can to keep others from enlisting. In these days all are patriots or traitors, to your country and to Jesus Christ.

---

7. William G. McLoughlin, *Modern Revivalism* (New York: Ronald Press, 1959), 410.

8. Ibid., 411.

9. Coleman, "Billy Sunday," 16.

Then Sunday jumped on the pulpit and waved the American flag while a band played and the crowd sang "America."[10]

SUNDAY'S METHODS

Billy Sunday took Moody's methods and extended them to new lengths. Moody advertised his meetings in newspapers, but Billy Sunday employed a public relations firm. Sunday enlisted a team of experts, which he called the "Sunday team" and took along with him on the road. His most famous assistant was Homer Rodeheaver, who became the best known gospel musician of the day. Rodeheaver served as choir leader, soloist, trombonist, and master of ceremonies.[11]

Sunday's revivals normally lasted from six to ten weeks and cost $30,000 to $200,000, depending on the size of the city. Most of the money from the nightly offerings went to pay the expenses of the crusade, but the last night's offering went to Sunday personally. Because this was widely publicized, Sunday received large "farewell offerings" during the years of his greatest popularity. For example, in Kansas City he received $32,000. His advance team usually arranged for a temporary tabernacle to be built in a central location. They put the famous sawdust on the floors to hold down dust and noise. During the meeting Sunday required that all the sponsoring churches suspend their services while the revival lasted.[12]

Sunday gained much of his fame from his athletic movements on the platform. The former professional baseball player kept himself in good shape, and he often preached while doing push-ups on the platform. Many people came to "see" Sunday as much as they did to hear him. He would run from side to side on the platform, sometimes demonstrating how to slide into home plate. He might grab a chair and threaten the devil with it, or leap on top of the pulpit to attack gambling. He even did handsprings on occasion. Amazingly, he continued to do these things even in his later years. Heywood Broun, the drama critic of the

---

10. Ibid., 15.
11. McLoughlin, *Revivals, Awakening, and Reform*, 146.
12. McLoughlin, *Modern Revivalism*, 423.

New York *Tribune*, wrote that Billy Sunday put on a better show than George M. Cohan: "George Cohan has neither the punch nor the pace of Billy Sunday." Sunday's actions offended some, but they kept others coming back night after night.[13]

SUNDAY'S RESULTS

The New York Times described Billy Sunday as "the greatest high pressure and mass conversion Christian evangel that America or the world has ever known." Sunday claimed that he had preached to live audiences numbering 100 million, and he reckoned that one million had "hit the sawdust trail." He held almost three hundred revivals during his forty years in the ministry. He claimed that 593,004 people came forward to shake his hand in his twenty most productive meetings. For example, in his famous New York crusade of 1917 the trail hitters numbered 98,264. The numbers are remarkable, even if some came forward more than once.[14]

Sunday enjoyed great success during his prime because of his colorful personality, his well-oiled revival machine, and his skill in reaching the middle class. He expressed the middle class' feelings and frustrations. Many of these felt uncomfortable with the social gospel and biblical higher criticism. Billy Sunday addressed those concerns and harkened back to simpler times. He spoke to those who preferred the "old-time religion." Many ministers who had difficulty accepting both Sundays' message and methods cooperated with his campaigns because they believed they were losing the battle with secularism.[15]

Eventually criticism wore away some of Sundays' popularity. Joseph Berry listed a number of these criticisms in a magazine article published in 1916. His objections included: (1) Sunday's attacks on pastors and church members; (2) the exaltation of the role of the evangelist and lack of recognition for supporting pastors; (3) the "shake-my-hand-method of dealing with inquirers; (4) overemphasis on statistics and their exaggeration; (5) the "vulgar display" of gifts presented to the revivalists by visiting

---

13. Ibid., 426.
14. Ibid., 415-16.
15. Ibid.

delegations at each service; (6) the high-pressure methods used to obtain his farewell offering.[16]

The most serious criticism against Sunday was that he made money from evangelism. He made no attempt to hide his opulent life-style. By 1918 he boasted that he had banked over one million dollars, and this boast deflated his balloon. His financial success estranged him from the middle class people who had supported him most faithfully.[17]

BILLY GRAHAM

GRAHAM'S LIFE

Like Billy Sunday, Billy Graham began his life on a farm. The son of a dairy farmer, Billy grew up just outside Charlotte, North Carolina. In 1934 a friend persuaded Billy to attend an evangelistic meeting conducted by Mordecai Ham. After struggling with the decision for several days, Billy walked the sawdust trail and accepted Christ. Within weeks Billy organized a Bible club at his high school and began to give his testimony at evangelistic services.[18]

In 1936 at the encouragement of his friends Billy Graham enrolled in Bob Jones College in Cleveland, Tennessee. After two bouts with influenza, Billy's family became concerned about his health and encouraged him to transfer to Florida Bible Institute in Tampa. When Bob Jones heard that Billy planned to transfer, he called him and tried to dissuade him. Jones warned:

> *Billy, if you leave and throw your life away at a little country Bible school, the chances are you'll never be heard of. At best all you could amount to would be a poor country preacher somewhere out in the sticks.* [19]

---

16. Joseph Berry, "Criticisms of Present Day Evangelism," *Zion's Herald*, 19 January 1916, 74.

17. McLoughlin, *Modern Revivalism*, 447.

18. John Pollock, *Billy Graham: The Authorized Biography* (Grand Rapids: Zondervan Publishing House, 1967), 7-9.

19. Ibid., 12.

During his years in Tampa Billy felt a call to preach and carried on an active ministry in the area. He experienced good results in youth meetings. In 1938 Billy submitted to baptism by immersion and became a Southern Baptist. In 1939 he was ordained as a minister in that denomination.[20]

In 1940 Billy Graham enrolled in Wheaton College near Chicago. There he met Ruth Bell, the daughter of missionaries to China. They married in 1943, and Billy offered himself as a military chaplain. The army advised him to go to seminary or get experience as a pastor. Billy accepted a pastorate in the suburbs of Chicago. During that time Torrey Johnson, a professor at Northern Baptist Seminary, offered to let Billy take over a local radio program called "Songs in the Night." Graham persuaded George Beverley Shea, a local radio executive, to produce the program and handle the music. They soon gained a sizable local audience.[21]

In 1944 Torrey Johnson gave Billy an even greater opportunity. Johnson organized the Chicagoland Youth for Christ and rented a theater next door to the U.S.O. Center. Johnson asked Billy to preach at the first rally. Over two thousand servicemen attended, and 42 responded to the invitation. Soon after, Billy was accepted as an army chaplain, but he contracted mumps and spent six weeks in bed. Johnson persuaded him to resign his army commission and his church and commit himself fully to the booming Youth for Christ ministry.[22]

For the next five years Billy Graham crisscrossed North America organizing Youth for Christ chapters and preaching in youth rallies. Youth for Christ rented arenas and stadiums for these area rallies, and Billy often preached to crowds of five thousand young people. Cliff Barrows assisted in the meetings and later became Billy's song leader and master of ceremonies.[23]

In 1949 Billy Graham conducted his first major crusade in Los Angeles. He attracted national attention when several show business celebrities and gangsters accepted Christ. William Ran-

20. Ibid., 23.
21. Ibid., 30-31.
22. Ibid., 32-33.
23. McLoughlin, *Modern Revivalism*, 487.

dolph Hearst sent a famous telegram to the editors of his newspapers instructing them to "puff Graham."   Graham soon had a national reputation. In 1950 he organized the Billy Graham Evangelistic Association with headquarters in Minneapolis. In 1954 he conducted a notable crusade in London, where he was invited to meet Queen Elizabeth. As the years passed, he preached crusades in every major American city and most of the world's major cities.[24]

GRAHAM'S METHODS

Billy Graham organized his evangelistic team and his meetings in the same way that Billy Sunday had. In fact, for a time he used an advance man who had worked with Sunday. Yet Graham learned a lesson from Sunday's handling of money. Early in his evangelistic ministry he insisted that he and all the members of his team be placed on an annual salary. All of the donations and honoraria he has received have gone to the Evangelistic Association which pays his modest salary. His financial integrity and moral purity have kept him from any hint of scandal.

Films. In July, 1950, Graham conducted a crusade in Portland, Oregon. Up until this time Billy had introduced no new techniques to evangelism other than the use of a lapel microphone and amplifiers. However, before the Portland meeting the Graham team asked Rich Ross, a producer of religious films, to make a documentary film of the crusade. This film, *Mid-Century Crusade*, was shown in churches and to religious groups across America. It brought Billy Graham to towns and villages. The Graham team used it to promote their meetings in cities targeted for crusades. Eventually, the team's film ministry became so successful they set up their own film company, now called World Wide Pictures. This company not only produced crusade documentaries, it also produced several fictional films with   evangelistic thrust. In all, Billy Graham's organization has produced more than one hundred films including *The Hiding Place*, the story of Corrie ten Boom.[25]

---

24. Sherwood Wirt, "Billy Graham," *New 20th-Century Encyclopedia of Religious Knowledge* (Grand Rapids: Baker Book House, 1991), 368.

25. McLoughlin, *Modern Revivalism*, 492.

The team. In the years after the Portland meeting Billy expanded his team until it reached thirty-five. Still, the key members remained the same: Grady Wilson, the associate evangelist; Cliff Barrows, song leader and master ceremonies; and George Beverly Shea, soloist. One measure of Graham's character has been his ability to retain the loyalty of his associates for forty years.[26]

Radio and television. In 1950 the Walter F. Bennett Advertising Agency encouraged Billy to begin a national radio program. Graham was hesitant to accept due to the expense but finally agreed when supporters donated enough money to begin. The program attracted listeners immediately, and by 1958 "The Hour of Decision" was heard by twenty million people each week. Listeners gave most of the money necessary to keep the Evangelistic Association going. Later the team often broadcast their crusades on television.[27]

Writings. Billy Graham has also touched many lives through his writings. He began writing a newspaper column in 1952. By 1975 "My Answer" was carried by two hundred papers. In 1956 Billy joined a group of evangelical Christians in founding *Christianity Today.* In 1960 his Evangelistic Association founded *Decision* magazine, and by 1984 it had a circulation of two million. Graham's books have also proven popular. His first book, *Peace With God,* sold over one million copies. Other successful books include *How to Be Born Again, World Aflame, Approaching Hoofbeats,* and *Angels, Angels, Angels.*[28]

Training. Billy Graham has inspired and trained others to evangelize. Each Graham crusade features a "School of Evangelism" to train pastors and ministerial students. In addition, Graham has sponsored three international congresses on evangelism: Berlin (1966), Lausanne (1974), and Amsterdam (1986). These congresses have helped the evangelical community focus on evangelism and discuss ways to improve the church's outreach.[29]

---

26. Ibid., 495.

27. Ibid., 492-93.

28. William Packard, *Evangelism in America* (New York: Paragon House, 1988), 226-27.

29. Douglas, "Graham."

Follow-up. Although Billy Graham has demonstrated a great ability to use mass media, perhaps his greatest contribution has been in the area of follow-up. Early on, the Graham team had to face honestly a criticism made of many traveling evangelists: Where are the "converts" after six months? Everyone agreed that many came forward in the crusades, but the team admitted they had a problem with follow-up. The team members counseled with inquirers themselves and encouraged the inquirers to read the Bible, pray, share their testimony, and join a local church. This approach proved inadequate as more and more people made decisions in the meetings.[30]

Finally, Billy Graham stated, "I have come to the conclusion that the most important phase is the follow-up." Without proper follow-up much of the effort of the crusade was wasted. To deal with this problem the team turned to Dawson Trotman, founder of the Navigators, a ministry to military personnel and students. Trotman and his associates, Charles Riggs and Lorne Sanny, agreed to design a follow-up system for the crusades. Their system involved several parts. First, they recruited and trained large numbers of counselors to talk with inquirers during the invitation. They also wrote literature to help the new converts understand their decision and begin to grow in Christ. Third, they set up an office in each crusade city. This office coordinated the follow-up for six months after the crusade, working with local pastors to ensure that each convert was contacted by a local church. These efforts have served as a model for other evangelists.[31]

ASSESSMENT OF GRAHAM'S MINISTRY

Billy Graham has provided a model for evangelists and leaders of evangelical ministries. His character and integrity are above reproach. His ecumenical spirit and positive actions in the area of race relations have aided Christian unity. He is without question the elder statesman of American evangelicals. His accomplishments speak for themselves. The question still must be

---

30. Pollock, *Billy Graham*, 103.
31. Ibid., 104-7.

asked, though: How effective is crusade evangelism? The answer must be: not so effective as it may seem.

Most persons who attend a crusade are already Christians. Churches bring their members in buses, and local pastors are exhorted to fill the stadium or arena with church members. Careful studies of Graham's crusades reveal that most of those making decisions were already members of a local church. Of course, this does not mean they were born again. It does mean, though, that very little church growth occurs as a result of a Billy Graham crusade. For example, in 1956 Graham preached a crusade in Glasgow, Scotland, and the team announced 52,253 decisions for Christ. However, only 3,802 people (7 percent) actually joined a local church as a result. After the Toronto crusade, the Evangelistic Association reported that 902 out of 8,161 inquirers had joined a church or intended to do so. The Graham team admits that 60 percent of their converts are already church members. They attribute the dismaying results to poor follow-up by local churches.[32]

What can we conclude then about mass evangelism? Mass evangelism is exciting, and it attracts lots of publicity. The best course seems to be to view crusade evangelism as a "seed-sowing" endeavor. It can be a good way to present the claims of Christ to the public. It can also serve to unite local pastors and excite church members. However, it should not replace normal church efforts to win the lost through educational evangelism, visitation, friendship evangelism, and home Bible studies. Mass evangelism can open some doors, but local Christians must take advantage of those opportunities.

ASSESSMENT OF REVIVALISM

Several factors combined to make revivalism popular in the United States.

■ The revival preacher's call to make a "personal decision for Christ" appealed to American individualism.

---

32. McLoughlin, *Modern Revivalism*, 516-18.

- Many local pastors supported revivalists with whom they differed theologically because they "got results." This is American pragmatism at its plainest.

- Revivalism promoted a religion of the heart. This emphasis appealed to the pietistic tradition in American Christianity.

- Successful evangelists put on a good show. During much of the period just studied, the revival was the best show in town, and it was free. With the advent of television the appeal of the revival meeting declined.[33]

One negative aspect of revivalism was and is that many churches confined their evangelistic activities to the brief period of the revival. They neglected evangelistic activities during the rest of the year. In fact, for many Americans revival and evangelism became synonymous.

The great revivalists did make the good news of Jesus Christ known to many people, especially city dwellers, who would not have heard otherwise. Perhaps their methods could have been improved, but at least they did something. The revivalists reached many in the cities who had become estranged from the institutional church. The evangelists lifted moral standards. Billy Sunday influenced the approval of prohibition, and Billy Graham contributed to improved race relations by insisting that his crusades be integrated.[34]

INTERPRETATION AND APPLICATION

Billy Sunday gained a large following in his prime, but by the end of his ministry he had become a caricature of himself. His platform excesses and love of money led many, especially America's intelligentsia, to have a low opinion of evangelists.

---

33. Richard Quebedeaux, *I Found It: The Story of Bill Bright* (New York: Harper & Row, 1979), 82-83.

34. Sweet, *Revivalism*, 171.

Billy Graham has made a significant contribution by making mass evangelism respectable again. His impeccable family life and handling of money have set a standard for others to follow. His skillful use of the mass media has also set an example that other ministries have imitated. His name has become synonymous with evangelism. Serious questions remain about the long-term effectiveness of mass evangelism. At worst, some see it as a waste of money and a distraction for local churches. At best, it is seen as an effective seed-sowing method, a public relations blitz. Thoughtful church leaders would do well to carefully evaluate whether the time, money, and effort expended in mass evangelism are cost effective.

STUDY QUESTIONS

1. What factors made Billy Sunday so popular?

2. What caused Billy Sunday's popularity to decline?

3. What innovations did Billy Graham introduce to mass evangelism?

4. Why is follow-up so important in mass evangelism?

5. What is your personal opinion about the value of mass evangelism?

~13~

YOUTH EVANGELISM

T he church paid scant attention to young people throughout most of Christian history. The church did not make special
efforts to evangelize young people. Instead, the church evangelized young people in the same contexts as adults. Concerned
pastors spoke with the youth of their communities just as they
did the older folks. At the camp meetings fiery evangelists
preached the gospel to young and old alike. However, in the
1800s groups of concerned Christians began to make special
efforts to reach young people.

THE YOUNG MEN'S CHRISTIAN ASSOCIATION

George Williams founded the Young Men's Christian Association (YMCA) in England in 1844. He aimed to minister to
young men in the cities. The YMCA promoted evangelism,
prayer, and Bible study. The YMCA movement spread to Canada
and the United States in 1851. In 1856 students at the University
of Michigan and the University of Virginia established collegiate
chapters. In 1851 the Young Women's Christian Association
(YWCA) was organized in England. It shared the same aims as
the men's organization.

The YMCA received a great boost when Luther Wishard was
named its first national secretary in America. Wishard worked
diligently to unite the scattered chapters. John R. Mott succeeded

173

Wishard in 1888. Both Wishard and Mott sought to convert college students and lead them to dedicated Christian service. Mott added a concern for world missions to the normal emphases on evangelism and discipleship.

THE STUDENT VOLUNTEER MOVEMENT

The YMCA and Inter-Seminary Movement combined forces at Northfield in 1888 to establish the Student Volunteer Movement (SVM) for Foreign Missions. The primary purpose of the SVM was to enlist college students for missionary service. Eventually, 175,000 college students signed a pledge to prayerfully consider becoming foreign missionaries; 21,000 eventually did serve as missionaries. The SVM adopted as its motto: "The evangelization of the world in this generation." The SVM achieved such popularity that at some colleges 50 percent of the student body participated.

The SVM continued to grow in numbers and influence until 1920, but it declined rapidly after that year. By 1940 it had ceased to be a significant force in world evangelization. The movement declined for several reasons. First, a number of changes in leadership caused the movement to lose momentum. Second, the economic depression of the 1930s caused serious financial problems. Third, many in the movement embraced the teachings of biblical higher criticism that subverted the authority of the Bible. Fourth, some SVM members suggested that social concerns should replace evangelism as the movement's primary concern. Finally, some feared that SVM represented and perpetuated western imperialism.[1]

DENOMINATIONAL STUDENT MINISTRIES

By 1900 the Christian denominations of the United States recognized the growth in the number of state universities.

---

1. William H. Breahm, "Factors in the Development of the Student Volunteer Movement for Foreign Missions" (Ph.D. diss., University of Chicago, 1941), 13.

174

Denominations sought to serve their youth and evangelize others by means of student centers. The Methodist Church established the first such center in 1913 at the University of Illinois. Other denominations followed their example and established student ministries around the country: Wesley Foundation (Methodist), Westminster Foundation (Presbyterian), Canterbury House (Episcopalian), Roger Williams Foundation (American Baptist), Baptist Student Union (Southern Baptist), and Lutheran Campus Ministry.

Usually, the sponsoring denomination appointed an ordained minister to direct the center and supported the minister through the denomination's budget. Some of these student centers merely provided religious activities for students who were already Christians. However, other student ministries, particularly those sponsored by Baptists, sought to evangelize students by means of campus revivals, dormitory Bible studies, and religious retreats.

INTER-VARSITY CHRISTIAN FELLOWSHIP

Like the YMCA, the Inter-Varsity Christian Fellowship (IVCF) began in England and crossed the Atlantic to North America in 1928. Inter-Varsity incorporated in the United States in 1940. This organization functioned on college campuses and focused its efforts on evangelism, discipleship, and missions.[2]

In 1946 IVCF sponsored a students missions conference in Toronto. In 1948 the conference transferred to the campus of the University of Illinois at Urbana. Since then, thousands of college students gather at Urbana every three years to study the biblical basis for missions and to learn about opportunities for missionary service.

Today Inter-Varsity has 750 chapters on college campuses in the United States. Inter-Varsity has gained a reputation for effective friendship evangelism and apologetics. The organization has

---

2. Keith and Gladys Hunt, "Student Organizations," *New 20th Century Encyclopedia of Religious Knowledge* (Grand Rapids: Baker Book House, 1991), 787-89. See also David M. Howard, *Student Power in World Evangelism* (Downers Grove, Ill.: InterVarsity Press, 1970).

accomplished this by sponsoring campus lectures by such evangelical notables as Paul Little, J. I. Packer, and John Stott and by publishing books through Inter-Varsity Press.

CAMPUS CRUSADE FOR CHRIST

North American college enrollment increased rapidly after World War II. The demobilization of the armed forces and the new "GI Bill" made it possible for many to enroll in college. A perceived need to reach these students prompted the establishment of a number of parachurch organizations. The largest and best known of these is Campus Crusade for Christ.

Bill Bright founded Campus Crusade in 1951. Bright testified that "God commanded me to invest my life in helping to fulfill the Great Commission in this generation, specifically through winning and discipling the students of the world for Christ." Bright sold his successful business and withdrew from Fuller Theological Seminary, even though he was close to graduation. He rented a house near the UCLA campus and began ministering to students. The first board of directors for Campus Crusade included Henrietta Mears, Billy Graham, Dawson Trotman (founder of the Navigators), and J. Edwin Orr. Within a few months more that 250 students, including the student body president and Olympic champion Rafer Johnson, had made professions of faith.[3]

Within one year Campus Crusade expanded its ministry to other campuses on the west coast. By 1960 Campus Crusade had a staff of 109 ministering on forty campuses in fifteen states as well as South Korea and Pakistan. In that year the organization acquired a defunct hotel resort called Arrowhead Springs. This facility provided a great headquarters and training facility. In 1978 Campus Crusade established the Great Commission School of Theology on the property.

From the beginning Campus Crusade demonstrated a commitment to aggressive evangelism. As Bill Bright stated:

---

3. Richard Quebedeaux, *I Found It: The Story of Bill Bright and Campus Crusade* (New York: Harper & Row, 1979), 16-18.

Aggressive evangelism is simply taking the initiative to share Christ in the power of the Holy Spirit and leaving the results to God. We make it a special point that aggressive evangelism does not mean being offensive; it does mean taking the offensive. Everywhere we go we tell everyone who will listen about Christ.[4]

Throughout its history Campus Crusade has maintained this approach. Campus Crusaders do aggressive (though not rude) confrontational evangelism rather than the friendship evangelism used by Inter-Varsity Christian Fellowship. Friendship evangelism (also called life-style evangelism) involves building a relationship over time so that trust develops and the gospel can be shared naturally and casually in a context of friendship. Campus Crusade also uses friendship evangelism, but their primary method is sharing their booklet "The Four Spiritual Laws."

Bill Bright uses three adjectives to describe aggressive evangelism. It is *physical* in that it involves going to people. It is *verbal* because the message of salvation is clearly presented verbally. It is *volitional* in that the witness seeks a willful response from the hearer.

Campus Crusade approaches each college campus with a four-phase strategy:

1. *Phase One: Penetration.* Staff members search for students with leadership potential. The aim of this phase is to develop a nucleus of student leaders.

2. *Phase Two: Concentration.* Staff and student leaders saturate one campus group with the gospel. Usually this is the freshman class. By winning freshmen the staff has time to disciple them and train them for leadership positions. They also encourage these discipled students to seek positions of leadership in campus organizations.

---

4. Ibid., 91.

3. *Phase Three: Saturation.* Campus Crusaders communicate the plan of salvation to the whole student body.

4. *Phase Four: Continuation.* The staff tries to keep the claims of Christ before the student body.Campus Crusade considers a college saturated when the staff cannot find anyone who has not heard the Four Spiritual Laws, when every group on campus has been contacted, and when surveys show that most students know how to become a Christian.

Campus Crusade has demonstrated great creativity in its methodology. Their basic approach to campus evangelism has been to use one-on-one witnessing, dormitory share-groups, and public programs. However, these common approaches have been supplemented with appealing programs meant to attract nonbelievers. These include Athletes in Action, a basketball team of former college players who tour the country playing collegiate squads and sharing their testimonies at half time. Campus Crusade also sponsors tours by Josh McDowell, an effective apologist, and Andre Kole, a magician and illusionist, who gave up a promising career in show business to dedicate himself to sharing Christ. Campus Crusade has also sponsored major conferences on evangelism like Explo '72 which was held in Dallas and attracted 80,000 participants and Explo '74 which drew 300,000 to Seoul, Korea.

In the 1970s Campus Crusade looked beyond college campuses toward the cities of the world. Beginning in North America, Campus Crusade sponsored the Here's Life campaign to saturate urban areas with the gospel. This involved contacting people by telephone and sending counselors to visit those who responded to the gospel presentation.

One common criticism of the parachurch student ministries has been lack of cooperation with local churches. Some local pastors have viewed them as competitive rather than complementary. Bill Bright requires all staff members of Campus Crusade to join a local church and encourages students to do so as well. Bright views Campus Crusade as a servant of the church. Campus Crusade staffers do not administer baptism and the Lord's Supper except in the context of a local church.

YOUTH FOR CHRIST

While Inter-Varsity and Campus Crusade sought to reach college students, other Christians founded parachurch organizations to reach high school students. One of the earliest of these was Young Life. This organization originated in Great Britain, and Jim Rayburn brought it to Dallas, Texas, in 1937. The disruptions of World War II brought with them an increase in juvenile delinquency. In response, a number of organizations were founded in the 1940s. In 1940 Jack Wyrtzen began holding Saturday night meetings in Times Square in New York. His Word of Life Hour attracted a thousand youth weekly, not counting those who listened on the radio. Later rallies drew as many as twenty thousand to Madison Square Garden.

Wyrtzen's success inspired others. By 1943 Saturday night youth rallies could be found all over the country. In 1944 Torrey Johnson, pastor of the Midwest Bible Church in Chicago, began the Chicagoland Youth for Christ. Its success led to the founding of Youth for Christ, International in 1945. Torrey Johnson stated the fourfold purpose of Youth for Christ: to reach every town in North America with the good news of Jesus Christ, to conduct citywide revival meetings, to help people see the lost condition of the world, and to reach the whole world in one generation.[5]

Billy Graham served as the traveling evangelist and promoter for the new organization. His charisma contributed to the rapid growth of the organization. Youth for Christ (YFC) also benefitted from the support of evangelical businessmen and the Hearst newspaper chain.

Bob Cook became president of YFC in 1948 and demonstrated considerable organizational skills. In the 1950s YFC organized high school Bible clubs (Campus Life) in order to better reach high school students. Campus Life also started a sum-

---

5. Mel Hall, *Youth for Christ* (Grand Rapids: Zondervan Publishing House, 1947), 130.

mer camping program. By 1951 YFC had held rallies in fifty-nine countries. In 1986 YFC had 1,065 Campus Life groups in the United States and ongoing ministries in fifty-six foreign countries. It also published *Campus Life*, an attractive magazine targeting youth.

In recent years YFC has suffered financial and leadership problems. It has also suffered membership declines because the number of youth has declined since the Baby Boomers passed through the education system. Still, the organization can point with pride to its ministry in juvenile detention centers and a thriving ministry overseas. Youth for Christ reported that twenty-two thousand decisions for Christ were made through its efforts in 1990. The organization is struggling to recast itself in light of the needs of American young people.

SUNDAY SCHOOL EVANGELISM

The parachurch organizations make an interesting study. They certainly have contributed significantly to youth evangelism. However, the venerable Sunday School has reached a lot of young people as well.

ORIGINS OF THE SUNDAY SCHOOL

Robert Raikes started the first Sunday School in Gloucester, England in 1780. A dedicated social reformer, Raikes established his school to improve the miserable life that workhouse children endured. Raikes taught the children reading, writing, and religion. Despite opposition from the Church of England, Sunday Schools multiplied. When Raikes died in 1811, four hundred thousand youngsters attended classes all over Great Britain.[6]

The first Sunday School in America was started in Virginia in 1785. The number of schools grew steadily, but Sunday School received its greatest boost when the American Sunday School Union was organized in 1824. This was one of several significant institutions spawned by the Second Great Awakening. Many of the

---

6. C. B. Eavey, *History of Christian Education* (Chicago: Moody Press, 1964), 225-27.

early Sunday Schools operated separately from the churches. Some pastors refused to allow a Sunday School in their churches because they doubted that laymen could teach the Bible.

Gradually the denominations began to see the potential for growth held by Sunday Schools. The Methodists and Baptists began to include Sunday School in their church programs, and other denominations followed their example.

The American Sunday School Union committed itself to evangelizing the Mississippi Valley by establishing Sunday Schools throughout the region. The Sunday School Union sent eighty missionaries to fulfill this goal. The most famous of these missionaries was Stephen Paxson. Riding his horse, named Robert Raikes, Paxson traveled through Illinois and Indiana starting Sunday Schools. During his ministry Paxson enrolled eighty-three thousand young people and established 1,314 Sunday schools. Scholars estimate that four of every five churches in the Mississippi Valley began as Sunday Schools, and in one year alone seventeen thousand people made professions of faith.[7]

Around 1900 Sunday School enrollment in the mainline denominations began to decline. Many of these churches viewed Sunday School as merely a means of providing religious education for the children of their members. However, the more conservative churches and denominations began to develop the Sunday School as an outreach organization. The Sunday School Board of the Southern Baptist Convention promoted Sunday School as the outreach arm of the local church.

FLAKE'S FORMULA

Arthur Flake provided strategic leadership for Sunday School development within the Southern Baptist Convention. In 1920 he was appointed head of the Sunday School Board's new department of Sunday School Administration. Flake soon developed and popularized principles of Sunday School growth.

---

7. Elmer Towns, "Sunday School Movement," *New 20th Century Encyclopedia of Religious Knowledge* (Grand Rapids: Baker Book House, 1991), 796-98.

Through his book, *Building a Standard Sunday School*, Flake laid out a five-point formula for Sunday School growth:

1. *Discover the prospects.* Flake encouraged churches to locate prospects and develop a prospect file.

2. *Expand the organization.* Flake discovered that starting new Sunday School classes enhanced growth because new classes grew faster than existing classes.

3. *Train the workers.* Flake taught the churches to plan for growth by enlisting and training new teachers for new classes.

4. *Provide the space.* Flake instructed the churches to plan for growth by providing space for new classes and projecting increases in attendance.

5. *Go after the people.* Flake emphasized visitation, insisting that planning for growth was wasted effort if Sunday School workers did not visit the prospects.

Thousands of churches followed Flake's formula and experienced growth. In fact, Flake's simple principles became the "Five Commandments" for Sunday School directors in the Southern Baptist Convention.[8]

Baptists made the Sunday School their key tool for evangelism. In 1945 J. N. Barnette wrote, "During the past quarter of a century approximately 85 percent of all church members, either by baptism or letter, have come out of the Sunday school enrolment. . . .The Sunday school is formed and operated for the purpose of reaching the lost."[9]

Southern Baptists have tended to point toward organization in general and to Flake's principles in particular as the key factor in their Sunday School growth. Elmer Towns discounted the role of organization and pointed instead to the evangelistic fervor of the pastors, commitment of the teachers, and dedication to the Bible as the important factors. Organization alone cannot

8. H. E. Ingram, "Arthur Flake, *Encyclopedia of Southern Baptists*
9. J. N. Barnette, *The Place of Sunday School in Evangelism* (Nashville: Convention Press, 1945), 24, 26.

account for the growth, but Flake's formula provided a simple and effective approach that enabled Southern Baptists to channel their enthusiasm.[10]

The 1970s brought a remarkable increase in Sunday School growth. In 1968 there were only twelve Sunday Schools of all denominations that averaged more than two thousand in Sunday School. By 1981 forty-nine churches averaged more than two thousand. Several factors contributed to this development. First, the 1970s was the decade of fundamentalism. Fundamentalist churches proliferated during this period, and they emphasized Sunday School attendance. For example, in 1981 the First Baptist Church of Hammond, Indiana, averaged over fifteen thousand for the year. The use of church buses also boosted attendance. A large Sunday School attendance became a matter of prestige among some pastors.

INTERPRETATION AND APPLICATION

Throughout most of church history, no specific efforts were made to evangelize young people. This changed in the 1800s. During this period the Sunday School and YMCA were founded to reach young people. Youth ministries multiplied rapidly during and after World War II. The founders of these ministries sought to win high school and college students and fill gaps left by the churches. No doubt these organizations did much good, but they also left some with the impression that local churches were ineffective in evangelizing youth. It remains to be seen if the churches can recapture the initiative or if they will surrender responsibility to parachurch organizations.

For their part, the parachurch organizations need to show a closer linkage to local churches. They claim to be servants of the church, but practical benefits of this servant spirit are often hard to find. The organizations report impressive numbers of conversions, but it is not clear how many of these converts become active adult members of local churches.

---

10. Elmer Towns, *The Complete Book of Church Growth* (Wheaton, Ill.: Tyndale House, 1981), 26.

STUDY QUESTIONS

1. Why did parachurch organizations take the lead in youth evangelism?

2. What prompted the development of denominational campus ministries?

3. What was Arthur Flake's formula for Sunday School growth?

4. What is a basic problem common to parachurch ministries?

$\rightleftharpoons$ 14 $\rightleftharpoons$

Personal Evangelism

Christians have witnessed for their Lord throughout the history of Christianity. Earlier chapters explained how early Christians shared their faith wherever they went. These first-century witnesses shared their faith as naturally as one friend telling another about a new restaurant. The Moravians, too, actively evangelized wherever they traveled. This type of personal evangelism was spontaneous. No one planned it or scheduled a "visitation night" on the church calendar. It is only in recent church history that churches have organized and conducted formal programs of personal evangelism.

Early Efforts

Dwight L. Moody used door-to-door evangelizing as part of his crusades in the 1870s. Other evangelists of the 1800s used the method from time to time. However, this method came into wide usage only after 1900.

In 1913 the pastors of Indianapolis decided not to invite Billy Sunday to their city. Instead, they agreed to conduct a three-year citywide visitation program. Volunteers from participating churches went house-to-house throughout the city. At the end of the effort the pastors claimed they had added twenty thousand new members. Similarly, in 1914 the Church Federation of Saint Louis launched its "One-to-Win-One Campaign." The campaign involved recruiting volunteers who conducted a religious census to discover prospects. During the second phase the pastors trained volunteers to visit and witness to nonbelievers. The volunteers asked prospects to sign a pledge to join one of the participating churches. The pastors visited those who signed the pledges. The Federation claimed that ten thousand new members joined area churches as a result of the campaign. The success of the campaign inspired other cities to use the same method.[1]

Naturally, professional evangelists observed the success of these campaigns. A. Earl Kernahan refined visitation evangelism to a fine art. He offered himself to pastors' alliances in various cities, promising to organize the campaigns himself. Kernahan lined up cooperating churches just as Billy Sunday was doing. He asked the pastors to recruit lay volunteers for the campaign. When the volunteers gathered, Kernahan gave them a pep talk, led them in singing lively hymns, gave them instructions on techniques, and sent them out in pairs to make their visits.

Kernahan gave each visitation team several "prospect cards" and instructed the visitors to write the results of their visits on the cards. Prospects who agreed to join a church signed a "Decision Card" and specified a date when they would join. When the visitors reported for duty the next night, they turned in their prospect cards to Kernahan or one of his associates. Kernahan reviewed the cards and reserved the difficult cases for himself. He then encouraged the workers and suggested solutions to problems they had encountered. When the workers had visited all the prospects, the campaign ended. The workers were responsible to visit those who pledged to join a church to ensure that they did so.[2]

Kernahan claimed remarkable successes in his many campaigns. He reported that volunteers under his direction visited 370,750 prospects between 1923 and 1929. Of these, Kernahan claimed that 185,8678 had been won. It is not clear how many of these actually professed Christ or merely joined a church. Still, his campaigns brought a number of people into churches.[3]

---

1. William G. McLoughlin, *Modern Revivalism* (New York: Ronald Press, 1959), 456.

2. Ibid., 458.

3. Ibid.

SOUTHERN BAPTIST EVANGELISM

Southern Baptists have been noted for their evangelism in the twentieth century. In the early 1900s Southern Baptists did most of their evangelism through revival meetings and Sunday Schools. All that changed in 1946 when C. E. Matthews left his post as Evangelism Director for the Baptist General Convention of Texas and accepted the same position at the Home Mission Board. Within months he developed an evangelism plan for the Convention which he explained in his book, *The Southern Baptist Program of Evangelism.*[4]

SIMULTANEOUS CAMPAIGNS

Matthews recommended that every Baptist state convention establish a department of evangelism, that local associations conduct simultaneous crusades, and that evangelism become a priority concern for every organization in the church. Matthews wrote:

> *We do not recommend that the soul-winning be done by a hand-picked group of trained workers; we recommend that it be done by every member of the church through our Sunday School, Woman's Missionary Union, Training Union, and Brotherhood. This should include the entire church membership. . . . [I]t is the business of the church to do the soul-winning, which does not end with the salvation of a soul but save the life in Christian service in the church.*[5]

The Convention approved Matthews's recommendations, and their implementation provided a great boost to Southern Baptist growth. The number of baptisms reported by Southern

---

4. Ronald W. Johnson, "Proposals for a Balanced Evangelism in the Local Church," *Review and Expositor* 90 (Winter 1993), 54.

5. C. E. Matthews, *The Southern Baptist Program of Evangelism* (Atlanta: Home Mission Board, 1949), 3.

Baptist churches exceeded the 300,000 mark for the first time in 1948. By 1955 baptisms reached 416,867, and the total for 1947-55 exceeded three million.[6]

Southern Baptists drifted away from Matthews's principles in the 1960s, and the baptism statistics declined. Baptisms decreased in part because evangelism ceased to be emphasized in all the church programs and organizations. Though church leaders talked a lot about evangelism, they did less than before.

LAY EVANGELISM SCHOOLS

The decline in baptisms and loss of evangelistic fervor alarmed officials at the Home Mission Board. In response, they developed a new program to involve church members in witnessing. The Home Mission Board and the state departments of evangelism promoted Lay Evangelism Schools all over the country. These schools used the WIN (Witness Involvement Now) materials to teach people how to witness. The materials centered on the use of a tract, "How to Have a Full and Meaningful Life," that was similar to the "Four Spiritual Laws." Those who attended the schools learned how to give their testimonies and how to use the booklet to lead someone to salvation. The school culminated in evangelistic visits by the participants.

Apparently, the Lay Evangelism Schools achieved their desired results. In 1972 Southern Baptist churches reported 445,725 baptisms, the highest total in Convention history. Unfortunately, the denomination could not maintain its momentum, and the number of baptisms began to drop. Then, the Home Mission Board developed a new program to reinvigorate the denomination's evangelism program. Impressed by the success of Evangelism Explosion, the Home Mission Board developed a new course of study called Continuing Witness Training. Openly modeled after Evangelism Explosion, this new program required participants to attend thirteen two-hour training sessions and actually to go out witnessing regularly. While the materials are

---

6. C. E. Willibanks, *What Hath God Wrought Through C. E. Matthews* (Atlanta: Home Mission Board, 1957), 123.

excellent, church leaders have had difficulty recruiting people to commit to a thirteen-week course of study.

CAMPUS CRUSADE FOR CHRIST

During the 1950s Campus Crusade had great success in personal evangelism using "The Four Spiritual Laws" booklet on college campuses. As pastors observed Campus Crusade's success, they requested training so they could use the materials in their churches. In response, Campus Crusade began its lay ministry program in 1957. By 1971 this had developed into the Lay Institute for Evangelism. The purpose of the Institutes was to initiate a multiplication program among lay people in the churches. Bill Bright and his staff hoped the lay people would win others to Christ, build the converts in the faith, and send them into the world to share the gospel.

In 1972 Campus Crusade sponsored an evangelism conference in Dallas called "Explo '72." This conference included evangelism training conferences, nightly rallies in the Cotton Bowl stadium, musical concerts, and a citywide door-to-door witnessing program. The conference proved a great success, attracting eighty thousand participants and resulting in five thousand decisions for Christ.

Encouraged by the success of "Explo '72," Bright and his staff planned a nationwide effort called "Here's Life, America." In cooperation with local churches they hoped to present the gospel to every person in the United States in 1976. That goal proved impossible to achieve, but in 1976 Campus Crusade conducted Here's Life campaigns in 165 cities in the United States and Canada. The campaign introduced itself to millions of people by displaying its "I found it!" slogan on billboards, television, bumper stickers, and newspaper advertisements.

The second phase of the campaign involved recruiting members of local churches to make evangelistic telephone calls. After training, these volunteers called the people in the local telephone directory and asked to present "The Four Spiritual Laws" over the phone. Those who prayed to accept Christ during the telephone conversation were visited by the volunteers, given follow-up literature, and encouraged to join a Bible study group in their neighborhood. Of course, the local pastors hoped those making decisions would eventually join a nearby church.

At first glance Here Life's statistics are quite impressive. By the end of 1976 volunteers from 11,826 congregations had contacted 6.5 million people and reported that 536,824 people had accepted Christ. Moreover, 60,000 had enrolled in the campaign's Bible study groups. Campus Crusade also estimated that 50 million people had viewed the television special prepared for the campaign.[7]

Though the campaign's statistics seemed good, the campaign drew criticism from experts on church growth. Win Arn noted that few of the converts actually joined local churches. For example, in Edmonton, Canada, 1,700 workers from 63 participating churches recorded 1,009 decisions for Christ. Only 250 of those people actually attended one Bible study, and not a single person became a church member as a result of the campaign. In Indianapolis 823 volunteers made 28,976 telephone calls. These calls produced 1,665 decisions for Christ. However, only 242 attended a Bible study, and only 55 became church members. Of these, 23 were transfers from another church. Therefore, the net gain in membership in area churches was 32.[8]

SATURATION EVANGELISM

Kenneth Strachan initiated the strategy labeled Saturation Evangelism (also called Evangelism-in-Depth). Strachan served as a missionary to Costa Rica and general director of the Latin American Mission from 1950 until his death in 1965. Dr. Strachan envisioned mobilizing all the Christians in a given country to evangelize their nation. He hoped to mobilize the entire Christian community in the nation and to evangelize totally the given area. To accomplish these objectives Strachan projected national evangelistic campaigns that would develop in four stages. In stage one a national conference would be called to share the

7. "Here's Life," *Christianity Today*, 4 February 1977, 522-23.
8. Win Arn, "Here's Life," *Church Growth America* (January 1977), 4.

vision with missionaries and national church leaders so as to gain their enthusiastic cooperation. Strachan described stage two as the mobilization stage. During this period prayer groups were to be organized all over the country. Once the prayer groups were functioning, training conferences would be conducted to train national believers in visitation and witnessing techniques. The plan emphasized door-to-door witnessing by local church members in their neighborhoods. The third stage involved parades and simultaneous crusades to be conducted in the population centers of the country. These would be union meetings supported by all the cooperating churches. Strachan projected the fourth stage as the follow-up stage. This involved local crusades, continued visitation, and discipling those who made decisions.[9]

Strachan implemented his program primarily in Central and South America. He and his associates conducted ten major campaigns between 1960 and 1968. The statistics for several of these campaigns are listed below. The net gain figures are the difference between a reasonable projection of professions for the year had no campaign been conducted and the actual figures for the year.

Country Net Gain Professions	Professions	Net Gain Professions
Nicaragua	2,604	624
Guatemala	20,000	4,800
Bolivia	19,212	4,608
Peru	25,000	6,000
Costa Rica	3,153	756
Venezuela	17,791	4,280
Columbia	22,000	2,832

9. George Peters, *Saturation Evangelism* (Grand Rapids: Zondervan Publishing House, 1970), 55-56.

In retrospect, Saturation Evangelism proved successful in producing professions of faith. However, it did little to increase church membership. Dr. George Peters, longtime professor of missions at Dallas Theological Seminary, stated that the campaigns did not produce substantial church growth. Why was there a discrepancy between professions of faith and church membership? Peters set forth several reasons for the problem. First, many experienced an incomplete conversion. These people came under conviction or showed some interest, but they were never born again. Second, some may have been confused in their motivation. Third, some Roman Catholics may have found professing Christ acceptable, but family pressure prevented them from identifying with an evangelical group. Fourth, the churches were not adequately prepared to do the follow-up. Fifth, the campaigns did not have an efficient method for channeling converts into local congregations.[10]

Strachan formulated a great and noble vision. He dreamed great dreams. Unfortunately, Strachan died before all of the national campaigns were completed. Perhaps, if he had lived, he could have changed his approach to enhance church growth.

EVANGELISM EXPLOSION

D. James Kennedy, a Presbyterian pastor in Florida, conceived and developed Evangelism Explosion. Kennedy was an unlikely prospect for the pastorate. Before he accepted Christ in 1955, he made his living as an instructor at an Arthur Murray Dance Studio. Kennedy trusted Christ after hearing a radio message by Donald Gray Barnhouse. Kennedy soon joined a local Presbyterian church and went back to finish his college degree. He graduated from Columbia Theological Seminary in 1959 and accepted the call to pastor a new congregation, the Coral Ridge Presbyterian Church in Fort Lauderdale, Florida.

When Kennedy began at Coral Ridge, forty-five people were meeting in an elementary school. After ten months the attendance had declined to seventeen. Kennedy's initial efforts at

---

10. Ibid., 74-75.

evangelism failed miserably, and he experienced great frustration. A pastor in Decatur, Georgia, invited him to conduct a series of evangelistic meetings. After Kennedy demonstrated his inability to witness to individuals, his host pastor demonstrated a method so effective that fifty-four people accepted Christ in ten days.[11]

When Kennedy returned to Fort Lauderdale, he began to go out witnessing by himself. Many people responded to the gospel, but he soon realized he could only do so much by himself. He organized witnessing classes of varying lengths, but they did not result in any conversions. Lay people attended the classes, but fear kept them from witnessing. Finally, Kennedy remembered how he learned to witness. Once he began to train witnesses by taking them with him, his program took off like a rocket.

Kennedy decided he could multiply his ministry by equipping some of his trainees to train others in witnessing. The trainees responded enthusiastically, but they wanted him to put his gospel presentation on paper. Kennedy kept notes on what he said during evangelistic calls for a month and then wrote it down. This provided the basic material that became Evangelism Explosion. The materials in Evangelism Explosion fleshed out Kennedy's basic principles:

- The church is a body under orders by Christ to share the gospel with the whole world.

- Lay people as well as ministers must be trained to evangelize.

- Ministers should see themselves serving primarily as equippers of the laity.

- Evangelism is more caught than taught.

- Training a soul-winner is more important than winning a soul.[12]

---

11. D. James Kennedy, *Evangelism Explosion* (Wheaton, Ill.: Tyndale House Publishers, 1970), 8-9.
12. Ibid., 2-7.

In Kennedy's plan trainees come to weekly training sessions for four-and-a-half months. They are expected to learn a portion of the standard gospel presentation each week. During the weekly sessions they spend thirty minutes in class, then they go out witnessing with a trainer. At first they only observe, but later they are asked to do part of the presentation. The whole presentation keys on two questions: "Have you come to a place in your spiritual life where you know for certain that if you were to die today you would go to heaven?" and "Suppose you were to die today and stand before God and He were to ask you, 'Why should I let you into my heaven?' what would you say?"

By 1971 Kennedy had trained five hundred people to ask the questions, and Coral Ridge Presbyterian Church had grown to 2,500 members. By 1977 it totaled 4,500 members. Evangelism Explosion became very popular, and ministers from all over the United States came to the church to be trained in the "EE" method. Later Evangelism Explosion went international, and trainers were sent to several foreign countries to establish the program.[13]

LIFE-STYLE EVANGELISM

In the 1980s life-style evangelism became popular among North American evangelicals. The most prominent spokesman for life-style evangelism (sometimes called friendship evangelism) has been Joseph C. Aldrich, the president of Multnomah School of the Bible. His books and tapes have popularized this approach.

Life-style evangelism is based on the premise that a person must trust the witness before believing the message. Aldrich reminds his readers that 80 percent of all new converts come to Christ because of a Christian friend or relative. Therefore, he contends that Christians must befriend lost people. Aldrich believes a Christian's holy life-style will attract lost people and bring them to the point of inquiry.[14]

---

13. Ibid., iii.

14. Joseph C. Aldrich, "Lifestyle Evangelism: Winning Through Winsomeness," *Christianity Today*, 7 January 1983, 13.

Aldrich points out that most Christians have no non- Christian friends; and, likewise, most non-Christians have no Christian friends. Thus the two groups seldom interact, and lost people have little exposure to the Christian life-style or message. Aldrich believes exposing non-Christians to believers with appealing, caring life-styles will improve witnessing dramatically.

In Aldrich's view evangelism is *being* more than *doing*. He sees evangelism as a gradual process rather than a project or program. He wants to see believers deliberately develop relationships with their neighbors so as to attract them to Christ. When non-Christians see the character and caring of Christians, they will want to become Christians also.

At first glance this might seem like "presence evangelism," which holds for maintaining a Christian presence and trusting that one will influence some to follow Christ. However, Aldrich's approach is much more intentional than that. He suggests praying for one's neighborhood and doing acts of kindness to develop friendships, friendships that will eventually lead to conversions. His idea is to deliberately befriend people with the hope they will accept Christ. He bases his approach in part on Paul's statement: "I have become all things to all men so that by all possible means I might save some" (1 Cor. 9:22).

Aldrich believes evangelism is a process that involves cultivation, which means establishing a friendship; seed-planting, which means sharing biblical truths; and harvesting, when the Christian appeals for a decision. To accomplish this, Aldrich suggests these practical steps:

1. Pray for your neighborhood and ask God to lead you to those in need.

2. Initiate social relationships by opening your home to other families in your neighborhood.

3. Build friendships through informal get-togethers.

4. Develop common interests in sports and hobbies.

5. Be sensitive to the needs of others.

6.   Look for opportunities to invite your friends to Christian programs and events that might interest your friend.

7.   Do not go too fast. Answer your friend's questions and proceed deliberately.[15]

Aldrich believes his method will allow Christians to share their faith naturally and without the stress and fear that come with other approaches. The many books, seminars, tapes, and videos dealing with life-style evangelism show how appealing his approach has proven in the evangelical community.

INTERPRETATION AND APPLICATION

In the New Testament era the laity witnessed spontaneously, but today pastors struggle to motivate members to witness. What was originally a way of life has become a church program to promote. Two truths stand out in this chapter:

1.   *Personal contact and follow-up are indispensable.* Many methods of personal evangelism serve well for seed-sowing. However, converts will only be incorporated into the church when Christians have meaningful personal contact with them. James Kennedy is right when he says that evangelism is more caught than taught. Most believers are afraid to visit, and this timidity can only be overcome through on-the-job training. Still, Kennedy's approach seems to work better in areas where there are single family dwellings and open apartment complexes. As Americans become more security conscious, door-to-door evangelism will become more difficult.

2.   *Most people come to Christ and to the church through a personal acquaintence.* As Donald McGavran insisted, we need to see new converts as "the bridges of God," people who can lead us to networks or webs

___

15. Ibid., 16-17.

of unreached persons. The first step, though, is to make the adult convert, who becomes the bridge. This will require intentional personal evangelism of some sort.

STUDY QUESTIONS

1. What aspects of Earl Kernahan's visitation method do we still use in church visitation programs?

2. What was the key part of C. E. Matthews' evangelism program for the Southern Baptist Convention?

3. What was the common failing of Here's Life Campaign and Saturation Evangelism?

4. What are the basic principles of evangelism as stated by James Kennedy?

5. What is the basic thrust of life-style evangelism?

6. Which method of personal evangelism appeals most to you? Why do you prefer it?

⊹ 15 ⊹

MEDIA EVANGELISM

The twentieth-century church has demonstrated a fascination with the mass media. Just as Martin Luther employed the newly invented printing press to enlist the German public in his reform efforts, so modern evangelists have used radio and television to broadcast the message of salvation.

EARLY RADIO EVANGELISM

The first public broadcast of a church service occurred on January 2, 1921, when KDKA of Pittsburgh, Pennsylvania, broadcast the evening vesper service of the Calvary Episcopal Church. In 1922 the mayor of Chicago, "Big Bill" Thompson, erected a radio station on the roof of the Chicago City Hall and invited the public to provide programs. A local pastor-evangelist named Paul Rader accepted the invitation and produced an evangelistic program. This may have been the first evangelistic radio program.[1]

Many people today mistakenly believe evangelical broadcasting is relatively new. Actually, evangelical Christians seized the opportunity to spread the gospel in the pioneer days of radio. The Moody Bible Institute of Chicago and the Bible Institute of Los Angeles pioneered media evangelism. By 1925 there were six

---

1. Jeffrey K. Hadden and Charles E. Swann, *Prime Time Preachers* (Reading, Mass.: Addison-Wesley Publishing Co., 1981), 73-75.

hundred radio stations on the air in the United States, and sixty-three were owned by churches and religious organizations.[2]

In 1927 Congress authorized the Federal Radio Commission to license radio stations and assign frequencies. The Commission discouraged religious stations because it believed commercial stations served the public interest better. The Commission assigned religious stations such undesirable frequencies and limited their hours of broadcasting so that only about a dozen religious stations were left in 1942. However, when FM band broadcasting became popular in the 1960s, the number of religious stations began to increase again.

The Federal Radio Commission's policy caused evangelicals to shift their programs from religious to commercial stations. Usually, they had to purchase time on these commercial stations. The stations gave free air time for religious broadcasts, but only to the Federal Council of Churches (forerunner of the National Council of Churches) and the Roman Catholic Church. The National Broadcasting Company established the following policy on religious programming: (1) Religious groups could receive free air time but should pay for production costs. (2) The programs should be non-denominational. (3) Network programs should use only one speaker to enhance continuity. (4) The programs should employ a preaching format and avoid controversial subjects. The network did not sell air time to religious groups, and especially not to evangelicals.[3]

Network policy forced evangelicals to experiment with innovative formats and develop fund-raising techniques. The Federal Council's programs were necessarily bland and slotted in undesirable time periods. The commercial stations sought to make a profit, and they naturally scheduled paid programming in the more desirable time periods.

CHARLES E. FULLER

Mutual Broadcasting System was the only network willing to sell time to religious broadcasters. Their best customer was Charles Fuller. After several years working in business and agri-

---

2. Ibid.
3. Ibid., 77.

culture, he accepted Christ and attended the Bible Institute of Los Angeles. In 1925 he started the Calvary Baptist Church. He broadcast the church's Sunday evening services from 1929 to 1933. During this period he broadcast another program called "The Happy Hour." In 1933 he left the pastorate to devote his full attention to his radio ministry, incorporated as the Gospel Broadcasting Association. Fuller's program, "The Old-Fashioned Revival Hour," was first broadcast nationally over the Mutual System in 1934 and internationally in 1941.[4]

Each broadcast began with the theme song, "Heavenly Sunshine." Then Fuller presented a simple expository sermon; a choir sang familiar gospel songs; and Mrs. Fuller read letters from listeners. This simple approach was certainly successful. By 1939 "The Old Fashioned Revival Hour" was carried on more stations in prime time than any other program of any type. In 1940 Americans heard Fuller's program on 456 stations, 60 percent of all the stations in the United States. By 1944 the popular media estimated his weekly audience at twenty million listeners. This is an astounding figure when you remember that the country's population was smaller then, and televangelists today are happy to draw an audience of two million viewers.[5]

NATIONAL RELIGIOUS BROADCASTERS

The National Association of Evangelicals (NAE) was organized in 1942. One of the NAE's concerns was to develop a radio ministry to compete with the Federal Council of Churches's broadcasts. To accomplish this the NAE set up a Radio Committee. This committee accomplished little, and in 1944 the NAE encouraged the formation of the National Religious Broadcasters (NRB). This organization promoted the establishment of evangelical radio stations and programs. Many of the stations established by NRB members were commercial stations with a religious for-

---

4. Earle E. Cairns, *An Endless Line of Splendor* (Wheaton, Ill.: Tyndale House Publishers, 1986), 218-19.

5. Quentin Schultze, "The Wireless Gospel," *Christianity Today*, 15 January 1988, 18-22.

mat. They meant to make a profit by accepting paid programming and enlisting sponsors for sacred music programs.

The growth of the NRB reflected the fundamentalist upsurge in the 1970s. In 1968 the NRB had only 104 members, but by 1980 it had grown to 900. The NRB's members produce 70 percent of the religious programs broadcast in the United States. Today more than one thousand radio stations and two hundred television stations with religious formats attest to Christian broadcasting's popularity.[6]

TELEVISION PERSONALITIES

By 1958 the United States had more television sets than households. The first preacher to capitalize on the rise of television was Fulton J. Sheen, a Roman Catholic bishop. His success on television fired the imaginations of preachers throughout the United States.

FULTON J. SHEEN

Bishop Sheen was no stranger to broadcasting. He had been the featured speaker on "The Catholic Hour" on NBC radio since 1930, and he continued to preach on that program until his television program debuted in 1952. His television program, "Life Is Worth Living," was broadcast live from the Adelphi Theater in New York City. Sheen made no apology about being Catholic; he wore his priestly robes, a red sash, a red skullcap, and a flowing red cape on the air. However, he delivered messages that spoke to people of all faiths and dealt with common human problems.

The DuMont television network broadcast Sheen's program at first. In the beginning only seventeen stations carried the show; but when ten thousand letters a week poured into New York City, Sheen's sponsor, the Admiral Corporation, moved the program to ABC. Sheen soon attracted a weekly audience of millions. His stately appearance, resonant voice, and stimulating messages combined to make him a media star. He received an Emmy Award for his broadcasts, and at the ceremony he joked, "I'd like to thank my writers—Matthew, Mark, Luke, and John."[7]

---

6. Ibid., 20.
7. Hadden, *Prime Time Preachers*, 82-83.

Sheen discontinued his program in 1957 because of pressure from the Catholic hierarchy. He resumed the program later but never regained his earlier popularity. Still, Sheen's remarkable success showed evangelicals that preachers with power and charisma could reach people through television.

ORAL ROBERTS

Oral Roberts showed the Pentecostal branch of American Protestantism what television could do. Roberts was born and raised in Oklahoma. Ordained as a Pentecostal Holiness preacher at age eighteen, he pastored small churches for several years. In 1947 he began his ministry as an itinerant evangelist. Like most evangelists of his day, Roberts bought a tent and conducted popular tent crusades for several years. His crusades featured healing services that attracted a lot of attention in the Southwest.

Roberts hit the big time when he began broadcasting his crusade services. After he televised his first program in 1955, his volume of mail increased 66 percent in thirty days. Then in 1969 Roberts developed "Oral Roberts and You," a weekly program filmed on the campus of Oral Roberts University in Tulsa, Oklahoma. This program featured attractive young singers, contemporary music, brisk pacing, and excellent technical quality. Roberts's brief message was the centerpiece of the show. By 1980 his program was the most popular of all religious programs, drawing a weekly audience of 2.7 million households. Four times a year Roberts presented hour-long specials on network television. These specials drew audiences of up to fifty million viewers and generated mail flow of 100,000 letters per day.[8]

TELEVANGELISM'S GOLDEN YEARS

The 1970s and 1980s proved to be the golden years for televangelism. Many evangelical preachers observed the success of Oral

8. David E. Harrell, Jr., *Oral Roberts* (Bloomington: Indiana University Press, 1985), 129; Hadden, *Prime Time Preachers*, 51; and Ben Armstrong, *The Electric Church* (Nashville: Thomas Nelson Publishers, 1979), 87.

Roberts and began television programs of their own. The most successful of these has been Pat Robertson. Robertson bought a television station in Virginia and began broadcasting in 1961. This station
became the first building block of Robertson's Christian Broadcasting Network. Robertson's talk show, "The 700 Club," achieved great
popularity. With donations solicited from viewers, Robertson bought
several other television and radio stations and a transmission satel-
lite. He was among the first to appreciate the impact of cable television, and he persuaded many major cable providers to include his
network in their systems. Robertson's winsome personality and business acumen helped him develop the Christian Broadcasting Network into the fourth largest network in the country.[9]

Pat Robertson's most successful disciple was Jim Bakker. Bakker helped to develop the original format for "The 700 Club," but he
was not content to remain in the background at Robertson's network.
Bakker introduced his "PTL Club" on a local station in Charlotte,
North Carolina, in 1974. By 1978 the program aired on over two
hundred stations. Eventually, PTL offered 24-hour programming
and reached more than thirteen million households. Bakker also built
a 2,300-acre theme park, Heritage U.S.A., which attracted 6.5 million visitors in 1986. Only Disneyland and Disney World drew more
visitors. The PTL organization received $129 million in 1986.[10]

As religious programs grew in popularity, other preachers
sought the limelight. Their programs varied considerably in format and doctrinal emphasis. They ranged from mainline Protestant Robert Schuller to fundamentalist Jerry Falwell to
charismatics like Jimmy Swaggert. While Bakker and Robertson
used the talk show format, Rex Humbard and Jerry Falwell stuck
with more traditional worship formats. All of them spent time on
their programs appealing for money. The cost for air time and sat-
ellite link-ups made televangelism a very expensive ministry. Still,
the televangelists did attract many viewers. These Arbitron figures
for February 1980 show the estimated audiences of the televangelists and how they ranked in the top ten religious programs.[11]

---

9. Armstrong, *Electric Church*, 101-2.

10. William Packard, *Evangelism in America* (New York: Paragon
House, 1988), 171-74; Armstrong, *Electric Church*, 109.

11. Hadden, *Prime Time Preachers*, 51.

Rank	Program	Preacher	Audience Size
1	"Oral Roberts and You"	Oral Roberts	2,719,250
2	"Rex Humbard"	Rex Humbard	2,409,960
3	"Hour of Power"	Robert Schuller	2,069,210
4	"Jimmy Swaggert"	Jimmy Swaggert	1,986,000
6	"Old-Time Gospel Hour"	Jerry Falwell	1,455,720
9	"The PTL Club"	Jim Bakker	668,170

Although the televangelists broadcast their programs all over the United States, their programs primarily attracted viewers in the southern Bible Belt and the Midwest. Again, the Arbitron figures for February 1980 show the regional popularity of the programs and preachers.[12]

Percent of Audiences by Region

	East	Midwest	South	West
Oral Roberts	10.3%	24.6%	53.9%	11.2%
Rex Humbard	14.7%	23.8%	46.5%	15.0%
Robert Schuller	24.0%	33.2%	30.1%	12.7%
Jimmy Swaggert	11.5%	23.0%	51.3%	14.2%
Jerry Falwell	12.9%	26.9%	44.9%	15.2%
% of U.S. population in region	22.5%	26.7%	32.4%	18.4%

---

12. Ibid., 60.

Even a cursory study of these figures shows that all the evangelists drew a sizable majority of their viewers from the South and Midwest. Roberts and Swaggert drew most from the South alone. Further audience research revealed that 70 percent of the audiences were older persons, that 60-73 percent of the viewers were female, and that the vast majority were already church members. The televangelists mainly preached to Christians rather than to the unchurched.[13]

AFTER THE FALL

The televangelists enjoyed a golden era that lasted about twenty years. However, just as the stock market crash of 1929 signalled the beginning of the Great Depression, the fall of Jim Bakker brought a depression for televangelism. The leading televangelists suffered declining receipts after the Jim Bakker and Jimmy Swaggert sex scandals of 1988. Reporters discovered that money solicited for missions projects had been used for other purposes. The lavish life-styles of the evangelists and their families disillusioned many donors with televangelists in general. Almost all the television ministries suffered loss of viewers and contributions, regardless of their integrity.

Jimmy Swaggert saw his audience decline from 2.2 million households to 400,000. Oral Roberts's audience dropped from 1,269,000 households in 1986 to 561,000 in July, 1988. Jerry Falwell's ministry went into a free fall, decreasing from 708,000 households in 1986 to 284,000 in 1988. These dramatic declines forced the televangelists to reduce their staffs and stop airing their programs in areas producing little revenue.[14]

INTERPRETATION AND APPLICATION

Media evangelism has become a major influence in American Christianity. In 1988 there were one thousand radio stations

---

13. Ibid., 61-62.
14. "Surviving the Slump," *Christianity Today*, 3 February 1989, 32-33; William A. Henry III, "God and Money," *Time*, 22 July 1991, 28.

and two hundred television stations with religious formats. How effective has televangelism been in winning the lost to Christ? Pat Robertson's Christian Broadcasting Network reported in 1977 that 41,500 were saved through contact with his network. Does a statistic like that validate the ministry? One can only wonder what was meant by a "decision for Christ" and how many of those people had made a previous decision.[15]

POPULARITY OF TELEVANGELISM

What has made the electronic church so attractive to Americans?

1. *The electronic church is popular because it is easy.* It requires little effort to participate or to maintain involvement.

2. *The electronic church is popular because it is individualistic.* There is no accountability to a pastor or group of Christians. No one checks attendance.

3. *The electronic church is popular because it is interesting.* The fast-paced, exciting, and engaging programs are certainly more fascinating than the services of the church down on the corner. One wonders, though, how much of the televised services are entertainment and how much inspiration.

4. *The electronic church is popular because it is successful.* What local pastor or church can compete with televangelism's millions of viewers and millions of dollars raised?[16]

PROBLEMS OF TELEVANGELISM

Thoughtful observers have pointed out several problems with the electronic church:

---

15. Wayne McDill, *Making Friends for Christ* (Nashville: Broadman Press, 1979), 10.

16. W. Robert Godfrey, "The TV Church," in *The Agony of Deceit* (Chicago: Moody Press, 1990), 167.

1. *Televangelism reaches few lost people.* Most viewers are elderly Christian women. Televangelists usually buy time on Sunday mornings when few lost people are likely to watch television. The high cost of air time forces the televangelists to stop broadcasting their programs in areas that produce few donations. One would think areas with lower numbers of viewers are precisely the areas most in need of the gospel. However, finances dictate dropping those same markets.

2. *Televangelism exalts experience over Christian doctrine.* Television does a good job of presenting images or pictures, but it does less well in communicating abstract truths. As a result, television's theological bent is toward communicating the experiences of believers rather than theological truth. When experience is exalted over sound doctrinal and biblical teaching, an impoverished and unbalanced gospel results. Televangelists are prone to interpret the Bible by means of their lives rather than interpreting their lives by means of the Bible. They talk a lot about what God is doing through "this ministry," while spending little time discussing the nature of God and teaching the Bible. The way the televangelists use letters and telephone calls from viewers reinforces their experiential bent.[17]

3. *Televangelism has little if any person contact or follow-up.* Televangelism fails to provide for the human contact new converts need. Even if the program succeeds in leading a lost person to Christ, the best the television ministry can do is to provide printed literature or a telephone counselor for the convert.

---

17. Quentin Schultze, "TV and Evangelism," in *The Agony of Deceit,* 193.

4. *Televangelism threatens to replace the local church with "the electronic church."* As long as the television ministry complements the local church, it is fine; but when the television program becomes a substitute for the church, that is a real problem.

5. *Televangelism often presents a sub-Christian message.* Most televangelists devote little time to teaching and biblical exposition. Their gospel is necessarily incomplete or even distorted. They sacrifice what is spiritually nourishing in order to be entertaining.

6. *Televangelism emphasizes entertainment and observation rather than worship and participation.* Participation is essential to true worship. Worship involves participation, but the electronic church cannot provide this.

7. *Televangelism causes viewers to judge their churches by unreasonable standards.* What local church choir can compete with Oral Roberts's singers? How many local churches could build a Crystal Cathedral? The electronic church teaches people to desire entertainment and to be dissatisfied with anything less than first quality.[18]

In conclusion, one must agree with Quentin Schultze:

We have seen that television and evangelism make for an uneasy marriage. The successful ones may never be the ones with high ratings, large audiences, numerous contributors, and state-of-the-art studios. Rather, they will be the ministries that support the local church, preach the biblical gospel, and avoid dishonest standards.[19]

---

18. Godfrey, "The TV Church," 167.
19. Schultze, "TV and Evangelism," 202.

STUDY QUESTIONS

1. Who was the first great evangelical radio broadcaster?

2. Who were the first two popular television preachers?

3. What made Oral Roberts's later program so popular?

4. What caused the decline in popularity of televangelists?

5. What are the strengths of television evangelism?

6. What are the problems with television evangelism?